PRETTY WRECKED

Confessions of a Teen Addict and Her Road to Recovery

Tracy Viola

Pretty Wrecked

Confessions of a Teen Addict and Her Road to Recovery

By Tracy Viola

Copyright © 2023 Tracy Viola. All Rights Reserved.
Printed in the United States.

Published by TEV Consulting, Wayne, PA

www.tracyviolaauthor.com

ISBN: 979-8-218-31721-8

|| DEDICATION ||

For anyone anywhere looking for a little light in the darkness of alcoholism and addiction: May this book help you to see something new.

For my mom, Jim, Al and all the people who helped me get – and stay – sober for over 27 years. *Thank You* will never be enough.

For my powerful girls. You will fall and it will hurt. I will be here – always. But more importantly, I hope I have shown you how to be there for yourselves.

For Mike. Every laugh, every adventure, every kiss, every day. You are my soul mate and the absolute best person I know. *Cent'Anni.*

*"Real change, enduring change,
happens one step at a time."*

~ Ruth Bader Ginsburg

*"You're entirely bonkers
but I will tell you a secret –
all the best people are."*

~ Alice in Wonderland

Table of Contents
~~~~~~~~~~~~~~~~~

ACT SIX: *I'm Still Standing*

Disclaimer: These stories are real and raw accounts of my experiences with drugs and alcohol. I had some good times ... but mostly bad times. In no way am I promoting or condoning any of this behavior or use of drugs and alcohol.

‖ PREFACE ‖

Why did I write this book? Why share these gritty vignettes and the dirty details of my brutal teenage plunge into serious drug abuse and my subsequent recovery from addiction?

Hope…. I'm writing this book in the spirit of hope. Plain and simple.

Witnessing the opioid epidemic and the increase in alcohol and substance abuse during and since the 2020 pandemic has been heartbreaking, shocking, even maddening at times. I know this suffering all too well.

I recognize and respect the fact that I am just one story. And I hope you recognize and respect the fact that I have been through some shit – some serious shit. Not only have I lived to tell the tale, but I'm grateful to say that since I got sober at 19 years old, I have thrived in recovery. While I would never wish any of the messed-up circumstances in my story upon anyone, I also know that I would not be the person I am today – a person I know, love and respect – without having experienced the hellhole known as addiction.

If you are reading this book as the rare someone that has not been touched by alcoholism or addiction in your past or present, I hope you find my terrible decisions both entertaining and cautionary. I hope you find the many skills I learned in recovery to be applicable to your life. Maybe an inspiration to dig deeper or to do something more as you strive towards clarity, peace, and joy (with a hefty side of badassery).

If you're reading this book because someone you love is struggling with addiction, your role is not an easy one, and I am sorry. I hope my story gives you a glimpse into this layered misery and offers some steps that can be taken towards recovery.

If you are reading this book as an active alcoholic or addict... maybe you know you are, maybe you think you are, maybe you feel like you've got this under control and you're not that bad. And maybe you aren't that bad... yet. In any case, I see you and I care. I know that empty hole that never gets filled and the feeling of desperation. And I also know ways to help overcome both. Please read to the end and I hope you will join me. For one minute. One hour. One day at a time.

"Be the change you wish to see in the world."
~Mahatma Gandhi

I'll go first....

My name is Tracy, and I'm a recovering drug addict and alcoholic.

Philadelphia PA
August, 2023

ACT ONE

~~~~~~~~~~~~~~~~~

Sweet Dreams

|| NOW AND THEN ||

January 1996

It was late and cold. I tried to get comfortable in the back seat of the empty car. I had finally found one in the parking lot that happened to be unlocked. I knew that this part of town was generally safe. I had no idea if the owner of the car would be returning before dawn, but I was out of options. I couldn't go home – I would just have to risk it and hope for the best.

I pulled some clothes out of my suitcase and arranged them on top of myself to get warm. Fuck it was cold! And between the fear of getting caught and the chill of the night, I wasn't sure how well I was going to sleep. So yeah, maybe signing myself out of rehab hadn't been the best idea – but it was too late to reconsider. At least I'd been able to leave with my suitcase and stuff. So ...

"Where did I go wrong? How did this happen?"

Damn – there it was again. Over the past couple of weeks, a little nagging voice in my head had begun talking to me ... but I didn't want to listen – I wasn't ready to listen. So I told the voice to shut up and go away, unwilling to look at or think about the past four years.

As I closed my eyes to try to sleep in the back of that cold Toyota sedan behind the ACME grocery store, my head swirling with the usual assortment of drugs that had taken over my life, I began to slip off and away. Somewhere between being awake and being asleep, I found myself remembering my childhood – before the drugs and alcohol, before my awful stepfather, before I knew what neglect or abuse meant – I began cycling through warm memories from my youth and slowly opened my eyes in a much different place ...

July 1986

My eyes tried to open against the bright sun, squinting to look for the bird I heard chirping over the soft sound of the corn husks gently rubbing together in the breeze. Ah, how beautiful this place was – of course it would have been more beautiful if I wasn't inhaling the stench of chicken shit.

This was back when my dad, for a period of time, was running a chicken farm in rural Pennsylvania. I was 10, and it was my weekend to spend with him. Of all the places he had lived in since the divorce, this was my favorite, despite the smell. I loved running around in the open countryside, weaving my way through the corn fields, playing with his gray and orange striped outdoor cat, El Tigre Gato.

My dad never really made an effort to keep an eye on me, regardless of my young age or where he lived. He wasn't exactly the most mature adult. I didn't spend much time with him after my parents separated when I was six, and we really didn't have a whole lot to talk about. Usually, our first day together was kind of awkward until we got into the groove of things, but I always enjoyed having the freedom on his farm to run around on my own, and be with him without actually 'being with him.'

I wouldn't realize until I was older, but my dad liked to drink – a lot. And when he got drunk, he would often lose track of time and forget his responsibilities.

I remember one time we spent a day together on his farm where he had enjoyed some beverages throughout the afternoon. He lost track of time and didn't start cooking dinner until well after dark. He was actually a fantastic cook, and on this particular night he was making his special beef stew. As it got later and later into the night, with beer in hand, he kept letting me know: "It needs to marinate, it needs to marinate! We can't eat yet."

After watching some TV, I wandered around the house looking at my dad's odd knickknacks, most of which had to do with the water, sailing, or alcohol. And then I discovered something very interesting to my young eyes – naked ladies. In my poking around, I'd found my dad's stack of Playboy magazines. You can imagine my embarrassment – and HIS – as he came to find me after 9 p.m. to let me know that the beef stew was finally finished cooking. Our eyes met as I sat cross-legged with Miss June on my lap. He mumbled a simple *"Dinner is ready,"* and we never spoke of the magazines again.

During another summer weekend with him at his farmhouse, my half-brother (from my dad's previous marriage) and I were playing hide-and-seek one evening.

I remember running as fast and as far as I could, and then sitting down silently in the corn field to catch my breath and stay hidden.

At first it was very exciting, not knowing if at any moment I'd suddenly get found. And then time went by – a lot of time – and I still hadn't been found yet. I was watching some bugs crawling up and down a dead corn stalk when I began to notice how darkness and a chill were starting to settle in. At this point, I didn't care about winning the game – I just wanted to get home. I wandered aimlessly around in a growing panic, becoming completely lost in that tall, rustling, seemingly endless sea of corn. I started crying and eventually gave up, having to spend the whole night in that cornfield, alone and shivering and deathly afraid of gigantic bugs or lurking monsters that might be watching me.

An eternity went by, then – finally – the next morning, as the sun came up, I found my way to a local road where a passing car picked me up and drove me back to my dad's house. I don't know if he'd been afraid for me through that night or was just drunk and out of it – but he did his best to laugh it off. For my part, I tried to act brave, as if the lost-and-found experience had been a fun adventure.

I'm pretty sure my dad didn't tell my mom about losing me in the cornfield when he delivered me back home in Philadelphia that Sunday evening. My mom, as usual, immediately made me go upstairs and take a shower while she washed all of my clothes trying to get the chicken-poop smell out of them. She then served me a normal dinner at a normal time (unlike my dad), and later we climbed into her bed together to watch TV. We loved to watch MacGyver and Hawaii Five-O. When the theme song for Hawaii Five-O would come on, she and I would sit up in the bed and pretend to paddle an outrigger canoe – I can still hum that catchy tune.

After TV, my dog Ruffles and I headed up to my bedroom. Ruffles often slept facing my bedroom door as if standing guard. She was a medium-sized mutt with wavy white hair – we named her Ruffles because her kinky hair looked like the ridges on a Ruffles potato chip. She was a rescue dog, and I suspect that Ruffles knew she had been saved by our family, and she treated us like royalty.

I recall the mornings without school where Ruffles and I would often run around the open space in our backyard, me still in my Wonder Woman pajama set. We didn't live in a rural setting like my dad, but we did have a spacious and secluded backyard, complete with a swing-set straight out of the 1980s. It had a metal slide which burned the backs of my thighs and swings with metal chains which pinched the skin on my hands and fingers. It was the best!

And after playing, my mom called me inside for a 'healthy' breakfast of Frosted Flakes or Cap'n Crunch. I watched The Smurfs and then went up to my room to play for hours with my Barbies in my huge Barbie dollhouse – and yes, I would make Barbie and Ken make-out.

*I would have given just about anything to get back into the
warmth and safety of my childhood room. Instead, I was
lying in the cold backseat of that dingy Toyota. I thought
about my mom and the violent argument we had on the
phone before I bailed on rehab. I thought about my sweet,
innocent grandparents who had taken my mom and I into
their home on that fateful day. I imagined they were sitting
together on their loveseat, probably watching yet another
rerun of the Laurence Welk Show right now. I thought
about how much I'd love to curl up with Ruffles and pet her
wavy, white fur. I was so alone ... I would have given
anything to feel her love wash over me. But instead, here I
was, only 6 months after graduating high school, just trying
to survive. My thoughts then flashed to another back seat:
my mom's 1986 Volvo Wagon...*

That car must have weighed 10,000 pounds, which was
good because I'm sure we hardly ever used seatbelts in
1986. I was sitting next to my best childhood friend, Juan,
both of us excited to go see the new animated movie, *An
American Tail.*

Juan and I wanted to sit separately from my mom in the
theater – we were, after all, 10 years old. We felt very
mature sitting in our own seats... until the scene where
Fievel the Mouse was lost, separated from his family, and
he sang the touching ballad "Somewhere Out There." Juan
and I quietly crept over to sit with my mom – the three of
us crying our eyes out while trying to share two tissues

she had pulled from her purse. To this day, I cannot hear one damn note of that song without wailing.

From ages six to eleven, I have some vivid memories of those five secure, mostly harmonious years. I truly enjoyed this part of my childhood. Yes, my parents were divorced, and talking to my dad at scheduled times on the phone or seeing him for sporadic weekend visitations was awkward, but I can't say I remember it feeling particularly problematic or depressing. I had my mom, and friends, and a nice neighborhood, and the best dog in the whole world. I loved both physical play and imaginary play. I was soft, silly, kind, and confident.

And then, when I was eleven years old, my mom was introduced to Richard on a blind date...

Richard would turn out to be a liar, con artist, and sociopath. And his poison would destroy me, almost to the point of death.

Almost.

ACT TWO

~~~~~~~~~~~~~~~~~

Broken Wings

‖ THE THINGS WE CARRY ‖

"It's okay to look back at the past, just don't stare."

~ Benjamin Dover

Taking Mr. Dover's above advice to heart, I would like to offer a bit of backstory for some of the key players in this memoir in ten pages or less. Shouldn't be too hard since I have few authentic memories of my parents together – they divorced before I was old enough to remember much. But the foundations of who I would become were laid in their own histories. Their stories became my story: I inherited a lot from each of them – their strengths and shortcomings, their joys and ordeals. So, who were they?

DAD

My dad was born in 1928 in the Philadelphia suburbs with two sisters and a brother. My understanding is that his mother was rather cruel, always telling him that he wasn't good enough and bossing him around. She even encouraged (pushed) him into his first marriage, which ended quite painfully. After four children, they separated, and my father's first wife sadly took her own life. A few years later he married my mom... and then I came along.

Despite this gloomy history and having almost zero relationship or parenting skills, my dad had a lighter side I fondly remember from my youth. He was often very jovial – always the life of the party, boisterous and funny and quick to tell a joke. I attribute my sense of humor, vocal loudness, and being unafraid to get up on the table and dance at a party to his influence on me.

But then – on the flip side of the coin – there was his drinking. Although my dad's drinking never caused him to be overly obnoxious or to say or do cruel things, it did contribute to his being unmotivated or disengaged most of the time... one can only dance on top of tables every so often. And in retrospect, it was also probably his drinking during our happy times that caused him to be so boisterous and funny and jovial. I'll leave it to the therapists to speculate on whether my teen drinking and drug problem was provoked by his early boozer example.

According to my mom, my parents had a very passionate relationship but not a healthy one. All things considered he was a poor choice as a life partner. He was basically an eternal adolescent – and that left my mom to take care of me, in addition to trying to care for his motherless children. She definitely didn't need the adult in her life acting like yet another dependent. Looking back, it was no surprise she ended things with my dad when I was six.

Despite our ups and downs through the years, I am so grateful to have developed a really beautiful relationship with him in his final five years of life – a relationship filled with understanding, acceptance and laughter.

I miss you, Dad. I forgive you. I love you.

MOM

My mom grew up with her parents and older brother on the Main Line of Philadelphia – a wealthy suburb where I've also lived most of my life. She had an extremely close relationship with her mother, who taught her how to be a refined woman (wife) of the 1950s and 1960s. This included trying to be quite pretty (which she was), never showing her intelligence and wit to a man (which she did quite well despite being both smart and funny), and always being subservient to the male in her life.

Because her dad was rather successful in business, my mom wasn't driven to develop a career of her own, nor was it encouraged during those times. And when she went off to college in Florida, she returned home two years later with an engagement ring (but no college degree).

That relationship ended within a couple of years – luckily without producing any offspring. She moved back to the Philadelphia suburbs where her father helped to support her. She worked miscellaneous jobs and had a few romances for seven years until being introduced to my dad, who literally looked like Robert Redford. My dad was, and I say this without trying to be gross, a total hottie – very good-looking and loads of fun. Maybe too much fun...

But my dad came with the previously mentioned serious baggage from his first marriage. My mom, for some crazy reason, decided to marry this man with four children, and a year or so later they added me to the party.

I came into the world with four half-siblings. Though the two eldest sisters had left the house by the time I showed up, I grew particularly close to my youngest half-sister, who was twelve years older than me. In many ways, she became my second mom as I grew up and, along with my half-brother, we shared good sibling times together.

When my mom divorced my dad, my closest half-sister and half-brother chose to stay with us instead of my dad. I guess some part of them knew their chances in life would be much better with my mom – and they were right. She did a beautiful job raising them. She was kind, nurturing, generous, and trusting.

Alas, these fine qualities would bite her in the ass when it came to my stepfather – and her very own daughter.

RICHARD

Richard was my stepfather, an ill-fated stain on my life from the ages of 12 to 16. He is not something I want to carry with me – but the reality is that he is part of my story, painfully woven into the fabric, an instrumental piece in all that was to come. Richard was a monster.

My mom married my stepfather in 1988 when I was 12 years old. Mom's courtship and wedding had been quick. After six years as a single mother, I think she wanted to be with and dote on a man – after all, that's what she'd been trained for. Additionally, I'm sure she wanted me to have a live-in father since my biological dad was not present nor reliable.

Richard initially seemed pretty cool. He was an airline pilot with a hideaway mountain home and fancy cars – a hunter-green Jaguar and a silver Rolls Royce, to name my favorites. (Years later, during the divorce, we would find out that his supposed 'wealth' came from scams he ran through his shady used car business). Things with Richard started out great. I was thrilled to have a father figure in my life, and for a time I think I naively loved him.

But within a few months of Richard living with us, he began to show his true colors. I heard him make obsessive demands about things around the house – what specific dinners he expected my mom to make, the endless snacks he wanted stocked in the pantry, what he hated about the décor of our home. Eventually he began demeaning my mom with increasing regularity, tossing cutting words at her at the slightest annoyance. Years later I learned that Richard actually forced my mom to make my half-sister move out because she wasn't her 'real' daughter.

In the beginning I did not receive the same harsh treatment because I was still an adorable, peaches n' cream, 'thank heaven for little girls' kid. But kids grow up, and that's when he started to turn his attention to me. His quips – subtle and silly, at first – became cruel and belittling comments. Unfortunately, I was at that vulnerable age where each of these critiques dealt a striking blow to my spirit and self-esteem.

Though my mom and I eventually 'left' Richard, I don't feel like I ever fully got away from him. I tried my best to silence his voice, but – as you'll see – my methods backfired, only hurting me and my family further.

|| 4th of July ||

Before my total crash and burn as a teenager, I fondly remember the great 4th of July parties my mom's parents used to host. They would spend weeks preparing the menu, purchasing the drinks and food, and decorating the house. My grandfather, who in his older years began to love yard work, would also spend every day outside tending to his gardens. By the time the 4th of July party arrived each summer, all the obnoxious weeds were gone and the lawn was immaculate.

They would invite all their friends and relatives for a backyard feast and pool party – swimming optional. My grandmother would make every item from scratch. Her hits included her famous potato salad (and let's be honest, who even likes potato salad?!) and a chicken salad that was the absolute best (the secret? Miracle Whip mayonnaise). I truly looked forward to these parties.

My grandparents' friends were always very well dressed and quite pleasant. Everyone seemed to be perfect – not one hair out of place, every female nail properly painted, and no one becoming too tipsy or loud. None of the adults would swim except for my grandfather. He had taken such good care of that yard and pool, there was no way he was going to miss an opportunity to enjoy it.

POP-POP

"Pop-Pop, let's go, let's go!" I would shout, grabbing his big hand in my little hand and dragging him out of the house, down the sloping lawn, past the guests and the food and my grandmother laughing at us, holding her VO on the rocks with a splash of water. I would jump into the water with pure abandon. But Pop-Pop would stand at the top step of the pool, put his hands on his hips and say "PHEW!" as if this was the first time he had ever dipped his toes in cold water. One step at a time, like molasses, he would slowly enter the pool. Finally, he would get in - blowing a big huff of air out of his mouth as if he was already exhausted - and play with me and my cousins. He would tell us what type of jump or dive to do off the diving board, and then judge us on a scale of 1 to 10.

Once we had tired ourselves out, we would wrap up in towels, still dripping, then run up to gobble my grandmother's delicacies – her delicious chicken salad and home-dipped chocolate-covered strawberries. I'd even sneak a Ginger Ale.

I have loads of memories and emotions related to my grandfather. Our relationship was never linear – it ebbed and flowed from loving each other to disliking each other and back again. We were probably very similar, and I was likely the first female to ever really challenge him. All the women in his life had been silent and subservient – and then there was me.

He was a self-made, very smart, old-time Philadelphia businessman who worked his way up to being a huge success. Thankfully the money he earned was able to provide a nice life for my mom and also helped offset my college education.

But with his success came exhaustion, impatience, and sometimes anger. My mom remembers how my grandmother would run anxiously around the house, getting everything in perfect order for when he would come walking in through the door after work. Mum-Mum would reapply her lipstick, wipe off the kitchen counters, and make sure his drink was made. As soon as he walked in, she would tell my mom and her brother: "Don't be loud, don't disturb your father – don't talk to him until he talks to you."

Despite being a powerful executive at work and a tough dad when my mom and her brother were little, he was always very kind to me as a child. Then, when my mom and I suddenly found ourselves living in his house, our relationship changed. My grandmother simply continued to run the house and be as charming as ever, but my grandfather was frustrated – and his frustration was probably warranted. I mean, his life was flipped upside down – he had to help his daughter go through another divorce, one that would last eight years in court, with endless paperwork and appeals. And he also had to watch his once-sweet granddaughter become a drugged-out monster right before his eyes. Unlike my grandmother and mother who typically wore rose-colored glasses, my Pop-Pop could see through my appearance and lies – he knew something was very wrong, and we fought often.

In hindsight, I think an underlying frustration of my grandfather's was that he couldn't control me. I would not be quiet when he walked in the room, and I would not happily apply makeup and wear black pumps.

It wasn't until years later that I could see that his anger and disappointment in me were because he loved me. My dad wasn't really there, my stepdad was a piece of shit – but my grandfather, as old-fashioned and frustrating as he was, had always showed up.

I'm truly sorry he didn't get to know me after I quit the drugs and alcohol. I'm sorry for a lot of things … but I'm most sorry about the last conversation I had with him. It will be forever seared into my brain. (We'll get to that soon enough…)

MUM-MUM

During those big happy 4th of July backyard parties, my grandmother would be the event's social butterfly – no time for the pool! She was engaged in chatting up her friends, re-applying her Revlon Fire & Ice lipstick, pouring the drinks, and making sure every bowl of food stayed full.

I wonder now what her feet must have felt like at the end of a busy day like that. I never once heard her complain, not about her feet, not about anything. I used to think she was superwoman – and as a parent now, I realize that *of course* she was tired or frustrated or in pain at times. She didn't always feel like making dinner and washing the dishes while we passively watched TV, then shouted into the kitchen for her to bring us something.

"MUM-MUUUUUMMMM!" I'd bellow to be sure she heard me over the sound of the sink.

"Yes, dear?" she would gently say, walking into the living room, drying her hands.

Smiling, I'd ask: "What kind of ice cream do we have?"

"Well, let me think – butter pecan, of course," (this was my Pop-Pop's favorite), "and mint chocolate chip."

I'd request some of each, which she would bring to me with haste before finishing the rest of the dishes.

Looking back, I am horribly embarrassed at my totally self-centered behavior, but on the other hand, I was still a child. I can see now that Mum-Mum had never been taught nor allowed to express her own needs or share her true feelings – she simply didn't have a voice. She was trained to please others and serve the man or children in her life. And she then passed these inherited lessons on to my mom.

I didn't say it then, but I can say it now...

Thank you, Mum-Mum, for all the wonderful times and your selfless hard work – for all of your efforts to make life easier for the people around you. I'm so sorry I didn't notice this or give you credit at the time. I have tremendous appreciation for you now that I see you through the eyes of an adult and a mother.

But I have to say, if I am doing dishes and my kids yell at me, asking for ice cream from the other room, I have no problem confidently yelling back at them: "Get it your damn self!"

|| Miss Teen USA ||

One afternoon in the autumn of 1990, when I was fourteen, I was sitting on the couch after school, and I heard my mom calling me: "Honey! Come see what came in the mail for you."

She handed me a letter with some writing plus a photo of a beautiful girl wearing a crown on her head. The letter invited me to submit an application for Miss Teen USA Pennsylvania. The girl in the photo at the top of the letter was Bridgette Wilson, Miss Teen USA 1990, who would later go on to be a wonderful actress in Hollywood. I sat there on our sofa feeling confused – and thrilled.

"But what is this – how did they get my address?" I asked my mom.

She stared at me, eyes wide, shaking her head. Neither of us knew – or cared. We were too excited! Of course, in retrospect, they probably sent this to every teenage girl in Pennsylvania – but at the time I felt very privileged and unique, thinking I really had a shot at that crown. My mom did as well, and we immediately went into planning mode.

The pageant allowed me to submit three to five photos along with a one-page letter describing who I was, what made me stand-out, and why I should be considered. Luckily, my mother was actually a wonderful photographer, something I wish she had pursued in life. So I got my hair and makeup ready, and prepared a variety of outfits to change into during our little photo shoot.

As for the letter, I remember writing and rewriting it. I had a particularly hard time with the 'stand out' part. I hadn't done many 'stand-out' things, especially compared to kids today. I look at my own kids and marvel at how many activities they're involved in at such young ages. And me back then? I realize now that I was probably a bit of a loner. I wasn't particularly interested in much outside of going to school, goofing around with select friends, and watching whatever was on TV at 4:00 in the afternoon – and of course catching my favorite music videos on MTV.

While I do not remember the specifics of the letter I wrote, I clearly remember the four pictures we sent in with the letter. One was a close-up shot of my face – so close that I thought my mom was taking a picture of the pores on my nose. Another was an action shot of me, walking and throwing my head back while holding a hat on my head. In the third picture I am crouched with my arm around my fluffy white dog Ruffles.

The last one was a glamor shot I had gotten at the mall a few months before receiving the Miss Teen Pennsylvania letter. Getting a glamor shot back then was a teenage girls' dream! In this magical photo, I'm wearing an oversized jean jacket off the shoulder, and on my head is a brown cowboy hat – plus giant fake-diamond drop earrings straight out of the 1980s-drama Dynasty. (I still have this photo!)

A couple of months later, we received a follow-up letter in the mail from competition headquarters and – I made it! I was actually being asked to compete in Pittsburgh the following March for Miss Teen USA Pennsylvania. My mom and I squealed and jumped around together in the kitchen. There would be lots of preparations to move through. The weekend would include three interviews with judges plus three photo shoots. One shoot would be of me wearing a casual outfit, another in a formal dress, and the last in a bathing suit.

The next five words out of my mom's mouth were (and are) her all-time favorite words – a question she and her own mother shared for their entire lives. *"What are you gonna wear?"* she asked in a high-pitched voice, her eyebrows up, eyes wide.

A delighted smile spread across my face. I admit that as a young teenager I used to love when she asked this question. It provided my mom and I with something fun to think about, discuss, deliberate. (Of course, as I grew up, this question would become less and less appealing to me, and time with my mom was something I began to increasingly avoid).

We had several months to get ready for this potentially life-changing event in Pittsburgh. Unfortunately, while my mom and I were immersed in deciding what I would wear, how I'd do my hair, what makeup to use – some comparatively heavy stuff started to come down on my teen head from my stepfather Richard. By this point he had been with us for almost two years, and he now fancied himself as the head of our household, a menacing presence that seemed to dominate every decision. His darkness – like a storm cloud – would always roll in to blot out my mom's sunny demeaner.

For instance, he would examine the photos of me and then declare that it was obvious I needed to get to work and prepare my 'questionable' body for the upcoming photo shoots in Pittsburgh. Up to that point in my life I don't think I had ever really thought about my body much at all. I'd always been slim enough and fairly strong, had nice long blond hair. I'd been excited to get my period at twelve, starting to feel like a big girl. And I admit that I was thrilled when my boobs began to appear quite nicely, if I do say so myself. I was vaguely into 'staying in shape,' occasionally going for a jog, listening to a mix tape on my cassette player – but only for a mile or two at a time.

"You need to lose a little weight to look real good in those photo shoots," Richard told me bluntly. "Especially in your thighs, look at them – they're pretty big. It's your lower body area that's the main problem. You need to get to work on that right away."

"Oh – well I guess – okay," I remember saying, feeling both confused and surprised. I'd never looked at my thighs quite like that before. I mean, they were just legs – and I didn't think they were THAT big.

My mom didn't speak up – didn't agree or disagree with my stepfather. Instead, she tried to turn Richard's criticism into something health-oriented. "Well," she said, "it certainly can't hurt for us to eat extra healthy for the next couple of months. And Tracy, you do enjoy going out for a run sometimes. Maybe we can focus on getting extra fit for this event. It could be fun!" Always the rose-colored glasses. Not a bad trait, but also not often realistic.

And while that's how it started, just a mission to be a little healthier and jog a little more, Richard would let me know in other ways where I was failing to meet his expectations. I'd be half-done eating dinner, and he'd say: "Tracy, you shouldn't eat any more if you want to shrink your chubby thighs."

The irony was that my stepfather was short, fat, and bald with a gross red nose from broken capillaries, telling me (a young impressionable healthy 14-year-old girl) that my thighs were too big and I should stop eating. And he was one to talk! He regularly decided to order himself a delivery pizza after my mom had made a healthy home-cooked dinner. Asshole.

But as he suggested, I would push my plate away and go upstairs to look judgmentally at my thighs and butt in the full-length mirror on the back of my bedroom door. Turning. Staring. Turning. Sucking in my stomach. Standing up straight.

I would try diligently to make myself run more and eat less. Actually, I thought I looked great – but there was now a tiny little devil forming in my head, telling me that I wasn't good enough, that I should do better, eat less, run farther tomorrow. And that same internal devil that Richard put in my head would get louder and louder during my teen years. (Unfortunately, it's been a voice I have never fully silenced.)

The weekend of the Miss Teen USA Pennsylvania competition finally arrived. My mom and I enjoyed the 5-hour drive to Pittsburgh. I remember lying on the backseat of the car, listening to tapes on my Walkman – The Police, Bon Jovi, Beastie Boys. Then I moved up to the front seat and practiced my speeches with my mom.

In my upcoming interviews, I planned to say that I was interested in becoming a psychologist. As a young teenager, my friends would often come to me for advice. I tended to be a good listener with a kind heart and gave decent guidance. This led me to be interested in mental health and psychology. (Interestingly, a decade later, I would actually become a mental-health counselor.)

After arriving at the hotel and checking in, my mom and I decided to go out to lunch before the scheduled events began. At lunch, I assumed we would eat something healthy, maybe a salad with grilled chicken or chicken and broccoli. When we sat down, my mom ordered us two iced teas. When they arrived, she grabbed a bunch of sugar packets and tossed them on the table.

"Do you remember Bermuda?" she asked, with a sly smile on her face.

She was referring to a short trip the two of us took to Bermuda a year prior. On that trip we ordered unsweetened iced teas and then dumped in multiple packets of sugar, which we sucked up through our straws and crunched between our teeth. Definitely not the healthiest thing to do, but a ton of fun!

Looking back on this moment in Pittsburgh with my mom now, as we giggled and sucked up that sugar, I think this was her small way of trying to rebel against Richard's body comments. On some level, she was trying to tell me that I was beautiful and didn't need to listen to him.

IN RETROSPECT

I did not win Miss Teen USA Pennsylvania – I didn't even place in the top ten – but it was an amazing experience and a weekend I'll never forget with my supportive mom by my side. The formal dress I'd chosen was a beautiful, long, red gown with sequins covering its puffy shoulders and bodice. Red satin hung straight down from the waist to the floor, with a slit up the back.

I have no idea why I kept this dress all these years, but it was just so majestic at the time I couldn't get rid of it. I was able to wear it again in 2022 for a 1980s prom-themed 'Decade of Decadence'. Yeah, that's right, I still fit in it. And I felt just as beautiful and magical in this dress at 46 as I did at 14.

|| The Washcloth ||

"Moooooooooom?! Can we please order pizza for tonight?"

Three of my besties from school – Beth, Lucy, and Caro (a.k.a. Caroline) – were coming for a sleepover at my house. We were all 15 going on 25, filled with confidence, cockiness, and a know-it-all attitude.

I continued, "And we're going to be downstairs making the cookies, too. Please DO NOT come into the kitchen when we are there!" I pleaded with her to not interrupt me, embarrass me, or even show her face in her own home.

"Sure, Honey," my mom sweetly replied. "Have fun. Let me know if you need anything." And then, of course, Richard had to add his little piece of advice, "Tracy, go easy on the cookies – don't be a pig." (Gee, thanks, Richard... that wasn't embarrassing at all...)

In addition to the obligatory sleepover pizza from Domino's (gross), for dessert we would be making my specialty: homemade chipwiches - vanilla ice cream sandwiched between two chocolate chip cookies and rolled in chocolate sprinkles.

While jamming to Top 40 hits supplied by the local Eagle 106.1 on the radio, we made the chocolate chip cookies while eating snacks and pizza. We ate so much of the cookie dough that there was barely enough to actually bake! (Screw you, Richard.)

After eating dinner and making a mess of the kitchen – which we obviously left for my mom to clean up – we went upstairs to my room for MTV and girl talk. I distinctly remember getting in the shower with Beth while we were fully clothed and singing pop songs into the shampoo bottles. Despite belting out Madonna tunes, I was wearing my black Motley Crue 'Dr. Feelgood' shirt that I had proudly purchased at Hot Topic in the mall. Lucy and Caro laughed at our karaoke and at the puddles accumulating on the bathroom floor.

After the silliness, we cleaned up the bathroom and decided to head outside for a walk around my neighborhood. But I knew my friends weren't just asking for a 'walk': it was something more...

I had started to dabble in things they were not yet doing. Because of my stepfather's cruel voice, I had begun to find outlets for my emotions through small rebellions. I was the first of the group to start wearing non-pastel-colored clothes, listen to hair-band music, and apply a bit more makeup. Plus, I had a couple of piercings in my ear versus the standard single pierce filled with beautiful pearl earrings. And I had cigarettes.

"Tra, do you have any cigarettes?" Beth asked, with a balance of excitement and hesitation in her voice.

"Yeah. So?" I said, trying to act nonchalant.

"Think maybe we could smoke some?"

I'm pretty sure Beth and Caro hadn't even been in the presence of cigarettes yet. Maybe Lucy had tried smoking once or twice, but to be honest I don't really think either of us were doing it right.

I think a little part of me enjoyed being the 'bad' one, so I was more than happy to bring the Marlboro Lights I had stashed in my sock drawer on our walk.

A bit down the road, I lit up a cigarette and passed it to Lucy. As I expected, she did that quick suck/puff thing - not inhaling at all, just basically kissing the filter. I'm not judging her – I inhaled, but I didn't like it. I mean, cigarettes are fucking disgusting. The only reason I was really doing it was for rebellion – it was the obvious next evolution of trying to be a badass.

Lucy went to pass the cigarette to Caro.

"No, I'm good," Caro casually said with both hands in her jeans pockets and her shoulders hunched up by her ears. She nodded towards Beth.

This was really all Beth's idea, so she knew she HAD to try it. And holy shit, did she try it – she took the biggest inhale I had ever seen! I swear she took down over half the cigarette in that one deep breath. I remember looking at her, coughing like crazy, eyes filled with water, face red, but also with the funniest smile on her face. I was surprised by how quickly she got herself together and asked for another drag.

"Sure!" I said, and we shared yet another cigarette between us.

As we headed back into the house, I was aware of the need for damage control. I stashed the cigarettes in the back of my early 1990s baggy stonewashed jeans, and we immediately washed our hands and started stuffing some food in our face to mask our stinky breath. In the cupboard Beth found a couple packs of HoHos, a fantastic cream-filled chocolate snack cake by Hostess (a type of junk food I would now destroy and throw out before ever letting one of my children put in their mouth).

After I felt like we had sufficiently covered our tracks, we headed upstairs to my room to start watching TV – the obvious choice was Beverly Hills 90210. We were split on who was hotter – Brendan or Dylan. I was Team Dylan... I loved that delicious rebel.

About fifteen minutes into the show, I noticed Beth was acting a little weird. "Hey, you okay?" I asked.

"Yeah, yeah. I'm fine! I think I just ate those HoHos too quickly," she replied with a forced smile.

"Okay, cool," and I shrugged it off, turning back to the TV. Although I wasn't really watching the show any longer, I was more interested in watching Beth slowly lose all color in her face.

Suddenly, she bolted for my door and ran into the bathroom.

Lucy, Caro, and I just sat there looking at each other, frozen in place, as we heard her violently vomiting. Do we go in and hold her hair? Do we give her privacy in this embarrassing moment? Will my mom or stepfather hear this and come to investigate?

Finally, we heard the bathroom door open.

"Uhhhhh, you good?" I asked Beth, who looked like total shit.

"Yeah, I feel a bit better. But I might need your help with something... ummmmm, come with me." Beth walked me to my bathroom and slowly opened the door.

Let me take a brief moment to mention what my bathroom looked like. While at this age I was slowly descending into a bit of a goth look, the colors of my bedroom and bathroom hadn't yet made the transition. My bathroom was decorated with a late-1980s light peach patterned wallpaper and beige colored towels. I need you to imagine the bathroom in a Calgon commercial – that's what I had.

And maybe it was the peach wallpaper that made the enormous splatters of liquid chocolate vomit look so violent. It was everywhere. Beth didn't just miss the toilet, she got it everywhere – the walls, the floor, the sink. I swear to God, that shit was on the ceiling. We looked at each other silently for quite a while. Lucy and Caro came running over to see the crime scene.

"NOPE!" Lucy said, hands in the air, and retreated back into my bedroom.

"Oh, Bethy! Are you okay? Can I get you anything?" sweet Caro asked.

I immediately grabbed the washcloth from the shower, still wet from our shenanigans earlier, and started to wipe her chocolate HoHo vomit off the wall. Off the floor. Off the toilet. It was me and that beige washcloth working our asses off for at least 30 minutes. Wipe, rinse. Wipe, rinse. That whole time I was terrified of what Richard would say if he came to investigate – I could almost hear the insults he would throw at me.

Finally, I finished cleaning her brown puke and we decided to go to bed after quite an exciting night.

This was the first and last time Beth ever smoked a cigarette. Her reaction was so vicious that it caused her to not smoke anything – not another cigarette, not pot, nothing – ever again.

I was not so lucky.

IN RETROSPECT

The notorious washcloth never recovered – it stayed stained from the vomit clean-up. I kept it hidden in my bathroom, and four years later I gave it to Beth at our high school graduation as a funny memory.

***

My first-born daughter recently turned fifteen. She took eight of her close friends out to a Hibachi restaurant for dinner. They laughed and screamed and took videos on their cell phones while trying to catch the shrimp thrown at their faces. After dinner, everyone came back to our house for my specialty – homemade chipwiches.

I hope we do the same thing for her 16th birthday. So very much can change in one year...

|| Against The Wall ||

And just like that, by fifteen I was well on my way to becoming the inexplicable asshole teenager that every parent fears, complete with a disdainful attitude, sharp tongue and solid eyeroll. I was wearing tight black clothes, blasting my music, postering my bedroom, and basically doing anything I could to establish a sense of independence.

I think some of my acting-out was just normal teenage rebellion. I was at the crossroads between being a child and becoming an adult. This was not a unique place to be – everyone goes through this weird transition while growing up. What made my experience unique, compared to the other teens in my school and neighborhood, was that I was enduring this delicate transition while facing the constant influence of a mentally and emotionally abusive stepfather.

My mom was equally a victim of this guy's dominance – something I didn't consider or appreciate until I was much older. While this shared harassment could have served to bring us closer, we instead let Richard tear us apart.

I remember one time when she was in my walk-in closet helping to put away my laundry – a task I would soon willingly take over so she wouldn't find anything hidden in said closet.

"So, whatever happened," she asked out of the blue, "to that Johnny something?"

I glanced at her without responding, my chin down, eyebrows raised.

"You remember," she went on, "you had a big poster on the wall of a 'Johnny somebody.'"

She was referring to my first-ever poster – my first celebrity crush. I loved *21 Jump Street*! I had that poster of Johnny Depp leaning on his elbow wearing that dark brown leather wrist wrap, white T-shirt exposing his Cherokee Indian tattoo on his bicep. Delicious! But at the time, my mom was very disapproving of Johnny. And so was Richard.

RICHARD & JOHNNY

When my stepfather married my mom in 1988, I was 12 years old and this was just about the time Johnny Depp had made his way onto my wall. As a young and innocent middle schooler, I enjoyed popular music on the radio and watching TV shows with my family. I still listened to my mom and was thrilled to have this new dad who paid attention to me.

But Richard's presence began to evolve – gradually at first, and then suddenly becoming an entirely different force in my life.

I had started to receive tiny critical comments from Richard about how I looked or acted, pointing out mistakes I had made. These were subtle at first, like maybe he was trying to give me some advice or guidance... but it escalated. And the advice became judgment. The judgment became criticism. And the criticism became abuse.

My first memory of being on the receiving end of Richard's verbal abuse was in St. Thomas where we flew down to spend a week on his boat. Yes, he had a small fancy yacht... in addition to his 4-seater Cessna plane, mountain house, and cool cars. (As I'd learn later, insecure men need a lot of adult toys to help make them feel worthy - all that classic overcompensation shit). While my mom and Richard went food shopping for our excursion, they left me on the boat to organize and clean the cabin.

Just before he left, Richard – the know-it-all – stopped and 're-tied' the boat to the dock. "These workers, they're so damn stupid, they can't do anything right," he complained in his superior tone as he quicky secured the rope.

Though I enjoyed the sun and the breeze whipping through my hair, I went down into the cabin and popped a Madonna tape into my Sony Walkman, fast-forwarded it to my favorite song 'Holiday,' and started dutifully cleaning the inside of the boat. I gleefully turned up the music and bopped around in the cabin, flipping my side-ponytail around and really having fun with the cleaning process.

I don't remember how much time went by, but a while later, I happened to look out the little window, and instead of the boat dock and marina, I saw nothing but ...

water. Out both sides of the windows, there were no boats or dock or marina at all – just ocean.

I hurried up the steps from the cabin and looked outside. In the strong breeze, the boat had somehow come unmoored and had floated off away from the marina. I could still see the dock, but I was now actually quite far out into the harbor. I started yelling, slightly panicked – but no one was around the dock to hear me. What could I do? I didn't know how to start up or run a boat!

Finally, I saw my mom and stepfather walking down the dock with a hand cart filled with groceries and supplies. I jumped up and down, waving my arms and screaming. My mom ran to the end of the dock and started yelling something, but I could barely hear her. Meanwhile Richard ran off to the dock office to get help.

Half an hour later I was being towed back to the dock. Richard was outraged at me. Even though I swore I had literally spent the entire time in the cabin of the boat and had not touched the rope, he was angrily blaming me. "What did you do?" he shouted. "Why did you mess with the rope! How could you do something so stupid? Stupid! Stupid! I'm so embarrassed by you right now... Stay out of my way."

My mom and I looked at each other, both of us knowing full well that he was to blame, not me – he'd obviously poorly re-tied the boat in his haste. But we would keep quiet, we would keep the peace.

Nonetheless I felt it – this new thing exposed. Different. Hard.

RICHARD & RICHIE

Johnny Depp was my crush in my pre-teen years, but during my transition to becoming a true teenager his poster was replaced with the Bon Jovi guitarist Richie Sambora – long dark hair teased to the tips, a few gnarly tattoos and a definite hint of a bad boy smirk to go with those deep dark eyes. I was growing up, and my bedroom was soon decorated with posters of musicians, purchased at the mall or ripped out of Teen Beat or Bop magazines.

As I began to develop my own personal interests and opinions, my stepfather more and more began to put me down, trying to 'keep me in my place.' At first, they were just occasional little comments thrown in here and there:

"You're only a kid – what do you know?"

"Keep your dumb opinions to yourself."

"Tracy, you keep quiet... Stay out of it."

"You could have done better on that test."

And my personal favorite: "You couldn't possibly understand this. You'll never know anything."

He could be so dominant and aggressive. Not knowing what to say or do, I often didn't defend myself. I learned to hold my tongue, scowl back at him, and walk in silent protest back to my room. To tune out Richard's voice, I would – instead – spend time with Richie, cranking up the volume and memorizing every note of his Bon Jovi *New Jersey* album.

Richard's ongoing criticisms became part of my everyday life and I didn't know any different. But something inside me – my sense of who I was – was steadily, if invisibly, breaking apart, like the gradual spidering of hit glass before it shatters.

Richard's verbal poison inevitably seeped deeper and deeper into the cracks in my soul – and the longer we lived with him, the worse things got. Richard became more and more cruel verbally and seemed to get off on it – even sometimes getting downright scary, acting seriously unhinged and out of control.

I remember one time listening to music in my room while doing homework after school. Richard came in without knocking, instructing me to pull weeds from the flower beds in the front of house. I let him know that I was just home from school, chilling out and getting some homework done, but that was not important to him. What was important is that the front flower beds were weeded – immediately. He stood in my bedroom doorway, staring at me with his beady eyes, silently pointing to the hallway. I grabbed my Walkman, *Slippery When Wet* cassette tape, and made my way downstairs and outside. He followed me closely, telling me exactly what he expected as I set up my cassette player, put on the gardening gloves, and popped on my headphones.

As he walked away, I said something under my breath - let's assume it was along the lines of "Dick" or "Asshole" or "Piece of shit." Because I had my headphones blasting music, I said it louder than I realized, and out of the corner of my eye I saw him storm over to me. The next thing I knew he grabbed my upper arm and was squeezing it while he pulled my face close to his. "What did you say to me? Huh?! You are just a stupid kid. You will do what I say, when I say it." He continued to squeeze my arm with his fat stubby fingers, making uncomfortable eye contact with me, until I was shoved back towards the flower beds to finish what I was instructed to do.

I was young and wouldn't have been able to fight back even if I wanted, but I was also aware that there was a darkness to Richard... something deeply malicious. I had a gut feeling that, for my own safety, I shouldn't even think about challenging him for fear of what he might do.

As a refuge I had my bedroom, my posters, my music... and Richie's dark eyes.

RICHARD & NIKKI

Otherwise, life went on – school went on, friends went on. I really loved my all-girls private school where I could arrive in uniform and brush my teeth and hair in the bathroom. No boys, no judgement, just my girlfriends – hanging in the Pepsi Pit or passing notes during class. I did well enough in school, not straight A's but a solid B average. And school allowed me to be silly and creative – I felt supported by both the environment and my wonderful sincere girlfriends. (In later years – even as I progressed further into my addiction – I would never mind coming to school... just as long as no one checked my locker for drugs). But maybe the best part of going to school was that Richard wasn't there.

Looking back, I can see that he was the worst kind of narcissist – totally self-engrossed, lacking any real empathy or morality, and projecting all his own buried insecurities onto Mom and me. I was too young and my mom was not yet able to stand up for us thanks to all of her 'keep the peace' teachings – so we just endured his abuse in silence.

To avoid Richard, I would come home from school and often go straight up to my bedroom, close and lock the door, turn on MTV, and wait for my favorite music videos to come on. When they finally would, I'd run over to the VHS player and push "RECORD – PLAY" at the same time so I could rewatch these videos over and over.

Richie and Bon Jovi were still a part of my life but, like my attitude, my taste in music had progressed. Now I was waiting for the bad boys of Motley Crue to come on the screen. I knew every word and every scene in all their hair-metal videos. The motorcycles, girls in leather, wild parties – this captured the storm brewing inside of me.

Bon Jovi, Skid Row, Metallica, Guns n' Roses – they were wild, loud, and extreme, not giving a shit about what anybody thought. I loved them, and still do. But by this time the baddest of the Motley Crue bad boys, bassist Nikki Sixx, was hanging on my wall. And it wasn't until my complete obsession with this tattoo-sleeved, flame-throwing, devil-worshiping, heroin-using rock god that my mom started to realize that maybe, just maybe, that Johnny Depp character hadn't been so bad.

RICHARD & THE SMELL

I remember one particular day in the Fall of 1991, continuing to be my moody 15-year-old self, blasting MTV in my bedroom. They announced a new video that was gaining popularity. I heard the first few chords and didn't think anything of it – until the drums kicked in. I turned my attention to the TV and watched this almost sepia-colored music video unfolding. The build of the song, quiet then loud, the crowd getting up and starting a mosh pit, the cheerleader gyrating with her pom poms and red "A" on her black bodysuit. *Smells Like Teen Spirit* by Nirvana was a game changer in the music world ... and in my world.

I sat listening to the song and watching the video, feeling something new bubbling below the surface. I felt the music overwhelming my core, exuding a different type of darkness. Not 'hair band' darkness – this was deeper, more emotionally dark, like out-of-control. And I remember feeling exactly that way myself, violently dark and ready to snap at any moment – wanting to dive into that mosh pit – not knowing how to take the edge off.

From Johnny to Richie to Nikki, I kept slipping into a worse and worse place inside, getting edgier, darker, angrier – a terrible but also natural progression down into an ever-growing curse of self-loathing. Almost inevitably I turned to drugs in a mostly unconscious attempt to self-medicate and ease my inner turmoil. Richard had lit a fuse. I was now smoldering, burning – and about to explode.

IN RETROSPECT

Who was I so angry at? Obviously, Richard – but also my mother. For years I would find my mom's failure of judgment and lack of voice or backbone against Richard unforgiveable. But with time, as I matured into an adult, I began to see my mom's situation more clearly. Her childhood training, cultural conditioning, and programming as a girl back in the fifties had been to stay forever controlled, submissive, silent – to be nothing more than a constantly beautiful and agreeable lady.

I would ultimately come to see that my mom wasn't purposefully trying to be cruel to me by having Richard in our lives. She hadn't intended for me to be harmed by the way my stepfather belittled and frightened me – she just didn't know how to stand up for herself. She lacked any effective tools in her emotional toolbox to address Richard's extreme and deviant behavior. Simply said – my poor mom just didn't know any better.

Was I immensely hurt by this experience? Yes. But I will also say that I genuinely love the person I am today – and like they say, perhaps without struggle there is no reward. The sword is forged in fire.

|| Little Black Dress ||

Between Miss Teen USA at 14 years old and my obsession with Nikki Sixx by 15 – so much changed in a year... including fashion.

On this particular Friday night, I was sure Mom wouldn't check under my actual clothes. And I had the backpack to throw her off – she'd check that, but not look under my outer layer of jeans and blue shirt to see I was *also* wearing the short little black dress I'd borrowed from Sasha. From my mom's perspective I looked like a quite normal and unassuming 15-year-old girl going out with my girlfriends to see a movie.

But there would be no movie with girlfriends for me that night. I was instead headed for a new teenage dance club called Baxter's. It wasn't a long walk from the movie theater where my mom would be dropping me off. The bummer was the money. In order to make my cover story work I'd have to buy a movie ticket and show my mom the stub as proof of my night out, and I'd also have to pay the cover fee at Baxter's. I just hoped they'd let me bring my book bag inside the club without making me check it for an extra fee – that would almost wipe me out of money.

"Oh, what do you have in your bag, honey?" Mom asked, as she casually looked in it.

"Ya know, just some snacks for the movie," I replied, not looking in her direction so she wouldn't see my worry. I actually did have snacks, but soon those snacks would be covered by my jeans and shirt stuffed into the bag.

At 15 I was well into my 'rebellious stage.' But this new dare of sneaking out in something I shouldn't be wearing, and attending a club I'm not allowed to go to – alone for that matter – felt like my first *real* act of treason against my mom's age-appropriate rules. Until now, my rebellion had primarily involved wearing lots of black, playing loud music, talking back, swearing more, piercing my ears – generally finding any reason I could to be down on the world at large. Woe is me. Poor little rich girl.

Yet despite these acts of rebellion, I usually tried to be a good kid out in the world. What's that saying? *"A saint abroad, and a devil at home"* (John Bunyan). I was polite to teachers and parents, I participated and did my homework – I hadn't even sneaked a drink.

Well, I'd come close – my neighbor Todd, who was about my age, came over with a friend of his one evening when my mom and stepdad were out, and he had a few sips of hard alcohol from our cupboard. I pretended to be cool with it and feigned taking a sip – but even doing that had been a little overwhelming for me at the time. I wasn't ready for that ... yet.

But there I was, waving quickly to my mom as she dropped me off at the movie theater. I rushed in to buy my ticket for evidence, then proceeded to the bathroom where I removed my jeans and shirt and wriggled down my little black dress. At the time I felt so sexy and mature ... but I must have looked ridiculous, like a try-hard.

I exited the movie theater and started the mile-long walk down Lancaster Avenue to Baxter's. I would need to time it so I could return to the theater, change, and be ready for my mom in the next two hours.

As I walked up to the front door of Baxter's, I could feel the bass of the music coming out of the building. I opened the door to darkness and laser lights - a fake fog filled the room, masking the people dancing. Unfortunately, I did need to pay to check my bag, which left me only a few dollars for a soda. I then stood there with my Mountain Dew, in my little black dress, just watching people.

I was not there with anyone to share this experience, my friends from school weren't into this 'scene' and I hadn't yet been exposed to a new crew. So I sipped my soda, walked around smiling and people-watching, and danced a little by myself. If I'm being honest, I was a bit underwhelmed by the whole experience. But still, I had done it. I had snuck out in my little black dress and gone to a dance club I wasn't allowed to go to. I might have been lonely, but I felt like a badass – and that felt good. Like it was my own thing, something I had that Richard couldn't control. A place where the music was loud enough to drown out his ugly patronizing voice.

And then, all too quickly, it was time to leave – to walk back to the movie theater, change into my clothes and go home.

To him.

‖ O'Malley and the 4-Leaf Clover ‖

"The real troubles in your life are apt to be things that never crossed your worried mind. The kind that blindsides you at 4pm on some idle Tuesday."

~ Sunscreen, by Baz Luhrmann
Written by Mary Schmich (1997)

It was Thursday, May 21st, 1992. I got up that morning, got dressed, grabbed some breakfast, and went off to high school. I was approaching the end of my freshman year and things were good(ish) in some parts of my life. I was doing well in school, I had friends, I had MTV and music, and I had just met a guy named Ponch a few weeks earlier – lots more about him later.

And so, feeling pretty good at the end of this school day, I took the bus home as usual and then walked casually toward my house. Everything was normal, nothing seemed out of place. I opened the mudroom door, still doing fine, walked in, and turned the corner to head up the stairs to my bedroom – but wait. What? The entire living room was missing. You read that right. The living room was just... gone. No couches, no chairs, no pillows, no television, no tables, no pictures. All entirely gone.

I gasped, looking to my right and into the dining room to discover ... nothing. The dining room was missing. No table, no chairs, no fucking thing where you store the china, no rug, nothing. In just a few seconds, but for what seemed like an eternity, I felt like I'd been transported into some alternate universe.

I'm not sure if I said anything. I don't remember if I called to my mom or if she came to me. But I remember standing in our now-empty foyer as she put her hand on my shoulder and said:

"Honey, we are leaving the house. Right now. We are leaving Richard. I called a moving truck this morning and had everything packed and sent into storage. We will go live with Mum-Mum and Pop-Pop in their house until I can find a place for us in the next couple of weeks."

She was making direct eye contact with me and her voice was surprisingly focused. Her words echoed in my head and right down into my heart – they literally echoed because the house was completely fucking EMPTY.

"Okay, okay," I think to myself, "this is good news, we're getting away from Richard." His behavior had recently become so creepy it was almost frightening. But – leave our house? Go live with Mum-Mum and Pop-Pop, like in their house? With them? Today? My mind was racing but I remained speechless ... in shock. How could all this so suddenly happen to me? This morning I had walked out the door for school and my living room had been there – and now it's not. I just stood there, not processing, seriously frozen.

"I've packed a bunch of your stuff in a couple of bags to get us through the next few weeks. I found your cigarettes but we'll talk about that later."

Shit. I suppose she did need to pack my socks.

My mom continued, "I'd like us to get going to Mum-Mum and Pop-Pop's as soon as possible. Why don't you go upstairs and double check your room and bathroom to see if there's anything else you want to bring."

It wasn't until right then that I heard the subtle shaking of her voice, saw the pinch between her eyebrows, her eyes just slightly filled with tears, her lips pursed.

I don't remember saying anything. I'm sure I said something like "Okay" or "How much time do I have?" or "Will we be back here?" But it's no longer in my memory.

I ran upstairs. My bed and things were gone. I opened my closet door and walked in. I had a pretty sweet walk-in closet with a lot of wall space which was plastered with my posters and magazine tear-outs. They were all still there, plus a bunch of clothes, jewelry, and souvenirs in the built-in dressers. But I wasn't focused on any of those, I just kept looking at my posters. I ran my hands along them, wanting to cry, feeling like I was almost leaving friends in my closet.

Instead of falling apart, I swallowed my tears and thought practically. I grabbed a few extra articles of clothing, some jewelry, and a few of the ripped-out 8x10 magazine pictures of the bad boys and bands I was obsessing over. But the posters stayed behind.

I helped my mom around the house with a few final things – packing a couple more boxes, moving our bags out into her car. Shortly before we left, around 5:30 p.m., a white van pulled in the driveway. The side of the van read "O'Malley Moving & Storage," which I recognized from the boxes I was helping my mom pack up.

A guy jumped out and said, "The other truck we packed up is already headed to the storage facility. I'm ready when you are, Ma'am, with your items in here," and he slapped the side of the van.

It was probably a month later that my mom told me what had actually happened on that day and why she'd reacted like she did. She'd had a session with her therapist a week or so before we moved out, and the therapist had very clearly explained to my mom: "So your husband has already destroyed you. Now he's moving on to destroy your daughter."

The deeply sad part was that my mom had apparently been okay with being destroyed – well, she wasn't okay with it, but she wasn't not-okay enough to do anything about it. But the thought of *me* being hurt by Richard was finally enough to get her thinking about getting us away from him.

But that wasn't actually the full story of why we'd suddenly moved. My mom then told me that Richard had left the house that morning very angry and mumbling to himself. She had felt seriously afraid of him – and when

she went into their bedroom after he left, she found –
what?! A handful of rifle bullets thrown on her pillow.
Read that again and imagine what your reaction might be
to that threatening image, both as a wife and as a parent.
What an extraordinarily terrifying and fucked up thing to
see on the pillow where you lay your head to sleep. In
response, Mom had called a moving company, O'Malley
Moving & Storage, who said they could be there that same
day to pack up the house and put things in storage for her.

Sitting in the back seat of my mom's white Volvo sedan, I
had my arm around our dog, Ruffles. All around us – in the
front seat, on the floor, next to Ruffles, in the trunk – were
O'Malley Moving & Storage boxes. Simple, sturdy boxes
with green writing and an image that looked like a four-
leaf clover. I held onto Ruffles in the backseat of the car in
5:00 traffic heading over to my grandparents' house ...
and just stared at those boxes. I wondered what my mom
had packed, what things were making the trip with me,
and what I had forgotten in the house.

I thought about how I had recently made friends with a
neighbor down the street and wondered when I would
see her again. I wondered how far away Ponch's house
was from my grandparents' house. I was falling quickly
for Ponch and was not going to stop seeing him just
because of the distance. And I wondered where we might
move in the next few weeks. Would it be a house, a
townhome, an apartment? I wondered if I was going to

really be in trouble for my mom finding the cigarettes ... or if this was punishment enough.

In the months that followed, every once in a while, my mom or I would need something and realize that it was in a storage box at O'Malley's. She would go there and try to find the box and bring it back to my grandparents' house. This was how I lived for the next three years – box to box to box – staring at that fucking four-leaf clover.

IN RETROSPECT

That traumatic move-out day is forever burned in my mind – but I guess realistically there was no alternative. How else could Mom have handled the situation? She did what she thought was best in the moment to protect me, to protect us. I would never wish that level of trauma on anyone, especially a child. But at the same time, as a parent now, I understand we sometimes must make impossible choices. I refuse to even imagine what Richard had planned to do with those bullets if we'd stayed in that house with him.

|| Mutation ||

"Mutation is the key to our evolution. It enables us to evolve from a single-cell organism into the dominant species on this planet. The process is usually very slow, taking thousands and thousands of years – but every few hundred millennia, evolution leaps forward."

~ X-Men Movie (2000)

It was a Saturday when the mutation occurred. We had suddenly left our home, fleeing Richard on a Thursday. On Friday I went to school in a daze. Then I came 'home' and unpacked my boxed belongings into the drawers that my grandmother, in her eternal patience, had emptied in her bedroom for our supposed 'few weeks stay.'

The next day – Saturday – it started to sink in. We had left my stepdad, a cruel, disgusting, abusive man. But we'd also abandoned our wonderful home, our neighborhood, my bedroom, my friends. Our whole world, our suburban house-of-cards, had suddenly come crashing down.

"I will never, NEVER, let this happen to me!"

I had stormed impulsively into the living room at my grandparents' house, and started yelling at my mom who was sitting in a yellow swivel chair. It was around lunchtime. My grandmother was in the kitchen making everybody a midday meal. My grandfather sat across from my mom in the other yellow swivel chair, talking to her about possible next steps. The sun shone in through the wall of windows – I could see down to the pool and the manicured lawn, but I felt anything but sunny and manicured. I was incensed.

"What are you talking about?" my mom replied.

"You! You are pathetic! You let this happen, you didn't do anything to avoid it. Why couldn't Richard leave – why couldn't we stay and he go? What the hell were you thinking?!"

I'm certain she replied and said something, but I was so enraged I couldn't hear anything.

"Now, Tracy..." my grandfather began.

"No, Pop-Pop – this isn't about you, stay out of it!" I yelled back impulsively. Before that moment, I imagine no woman had ever spoken to him in that manner. He sat there, shocked and silent, unsure of what to do with this unruly teenager who was now living for the foreseeable future in his formerly quiet, peaceful home.

My voice lowered almost to a growl as I continued shouting at my mom – and the words rushing out of my mouth would change my DNA and dictate my actions and choices for years to come:

"I will never allow anybody to control my life. I will always be in control of myself. I will always have my own money. I will never rely on anybody else. I will never, ever become like you."

Nobody spoke. I slowly and calmly walked out of the sunny living room, down into the dark hallway, and closed the door to my grandmother's bedroom -- now MY bedroom.

IN RETROSPECT

I remember the shift in my soul taking place. I felt like someone had cut the top of my head open and rewired my brain, then moved lower to wrap some barbed wire around my heart. I stopped being vulnerable – trusting others and letting people in was a fool's game. I began to assume I would need to meet my own needs – physical, emotional, financial – both as a teenager and into adulthood. I would keep my cards close to my heart and figure things out for myself.

It would take years of recovery and therapy before I removed most of the barbed wire around my heart. The rewiring of the brain, however... that has remained.

ACT THREE

~~~~~~~~~~~~~~~~

Dr. Feelgood

|| This Is It. This Is the Answer. ||

At thirteen, I was a wide-eyed, adorable marshmallow. By fourteen, the wool was slowly being pulled from my eyes. The cruel comments of my stepfather, coupled with the lack of phone calls or visits from my real father, had started to sadden me. My eyes were not as wide, and at times my youthful positivity would slip and I'd feel depressed.

By fifteen, the teenager in me was in full effect. I had a little devil on my shoulder offering valid reasons for why I should rightfully feel shitty. I was already starting to establish some sense of independence, breaking a few rules to test the limits.

But sixteen? The wheels would come off in my 16th year. Sixteen-year-old Tracy wouldn't even recognize thirteen-year-old Tracy.

The summer after I turned 15, I had my first kiss. It was a perfect first kiss with a boy I liked very much, in his Jeep Cherokee on a warm summer night after a lovely movie date. I was wearing white jeans and a blue shirt that had ruffles on the shoulders. The song 'More Than Words' by Extreme was on the radio for my first kiss. This boy and I would date for the next three to four months. We never got past second base, but I still remember those fun butterflies-in-my-stomach times.

I would kiss one or two boys after that first kiss, but I don't remember the details or the names. I certainly don't remember what song was playing on the radio. But I definitely remember the day I met Ponch in early May, 1992.

"Come over to hang out later tonight," my friend Cecilia had said to me with her beautiful European accent. "I'm having Bill and some people from school over. My parents are in Paris for a few days."

She was from France, and her parents would often be abroad for work or maybe family – I don't remember – but they would leave her alone at home sometimes for a few days. Alone. Mind-blowing, I know, but she was a straight-A student and involved in smart-people clubs at school, so I guess they thought they could trust her. (I would remember this bullshit that 'people with good grades seem more trustworthy' as I sank into my addiction. Even at my worst, I always worked hard to get decent grades – this meant I would be less likely to turn heads.)

"Ok," I said, "I'll try to come by after dinner."

Around 7:30 I walked over to her house, around back and through the sliding door into their kitchen. The song 'Stray Cat Strut' was playing and Cecilia and Bill were swing-dancing. Bill was a unique guy and quite a lovely dancer.

Cecilia smiled and waved at me upside down as Bill dipped her. I grabbed a stool at the kitchen counter and said hi to a few people sitting there. They had beers and wine coolers on the counter. I was offered one and took a beer. This was maybe the second, possibly third time I had tried drinking. To be honest I never really liked the taste of alcohol. Even in the depths of my abuse, alcohol would be my last choice.

As I sat there at the kitchen counter, feet swinging off the stool, pretending to enjoy my beer and watching Cecilia and Bill dance, a guy walked into the room.

"Coo, coo, ca-choo!" he said loudly and confidently – and everyone started to cheer and high-five him.

"Why's everybody congratulating him?" I asked the girl next to me who had clearly not been fake-drinking her beer like me.

"He just became our student council president!" she sang, eyes at half-mast. This guy was maybe 6' 2", pretty lean but with muscle. He had long, wavy, brown hair in a messy, low ponytail, with strands hanging around his face. He was wearing a very worn tie-dye t-shirt and khaki shorts.

He and Cecilia's boyfriend Bill hugged in greeting. Bill grabbed a hacky sack that was on the kitchen counter and they walked out the sliding door into the back yard. As this new guy turned to close the door our eyes met. Pause.

"Hey," he said.

"Hey," I said back, acting calm and collected on the surface. But my insides were like a little duck's feet, churning a mile a minute under the surface, my chest tight and short of breath.

He disappeared outside. I don't know how much time passed but it felt like an eternity. Finally, he came back in, and though he was trying to act cool, I could tell he was making his way over to me.

"I'm Ponch. You are?"

"Tracy. I live across the street."

"Oh, cool. You don't go to our school."

"I go to an all-girls private school not far away."

Every time I had to tell someone this, I'd kind of roll my eyes so it hopefully didn't come out sounding snobby. He nodded. Looking down and around, and then back at me.

"So where does the name Ponch come from?" I asked him, never having heard that name but thinking it was cool.

"My real name's Frank. My parents watched CHiPs and there's a character on the show named Frank, but they call him Ponch – they started calling me Ponch and it stuck."

"Oh, cool," I replied.

And after that I don't remember what we talked about. I just remember realizing it was way past the time I said I would be home – but I had to see this boy again. Immediately.

***

I guess it was love at first sight for both of us. We quickly became obsessed with each other, talking on the phone and spending any minute we could at Cecilia's house – parents or no parents.

I remember our first kiss – it was on Cecilia's patio about a week or so after we first met. We were standing there listening to music playing in the background, likely Pink Floyd or The Grateful Dead or Led Zepplin – those were bands Ponch was into. I was leaning against the back of a chair when he walked over to me slowly, flipping his hair back, then took my face in his hands.

He looked into my eyes, lifted my chin up, and kissed me with a soft closed mouth. I felt strands of his hair fall down and tickle my cheeks. We stayed like that for what felt like hours. Then he pulled away and looked at me intently – and for all the things that were to follow and the mistakes and life-altering decisions he led me into, I will never forget or regret that first moment of experiencing the tingle of true love.

One thing quickly became clear to me about Ponch. He was always pretty chill – he seemed genuinely happy and at ease pretty much all the time. This was not because he knew something we didn't or had some special meditation practice. It was, as I'd soon find out, because he was high all the time. That actually didn't bother me - I really wasn't interested in smoking pot, despite being around it ever since that first week I met Ponch.

Watching him, Bill, and some of the other people smoke a joint was the first time I ever saw or smelled pot. I'd been taught that drugs were bad – you know, the whole Nancy Reagan "Just Say No" educational campaign. But these friends of mine who smoked pot didn't seem at all like the strung-out outlaws the news portrayed. I didn't mind that Ponch got high, I was madly in love with him. He was joyful and kind and made me happy – something my life had been seriously lacking. I almost hadn't realized how much until I met him.

Then, about two weeks after my first kiss with Ponch, I found myself sitting in the back of my mom's white Volvo, clutching onto my dog Ruffles while looking at those goddamn O'Malley's Moving & Storage boxes. I thought about what I was leaving behind at my home, and I thought about being thirty minutes farther away from Ponch – would that make things with him more complicated?

But we made it work, thanks to my mom driving me to and from his house, his mom driving me, and his friends occasionally driving us as well. We would see each other at least every weekend, and then more often as May turned into June and summer vacation – Ponch became my weekly bit of total delight.

After dating and being madly in love for two months, the physical aspects of our relationship had progressed to where, in July of 1992, we had sex. I was a virgin, he was not. He was wonderful and patient. I truly loved him.

I wore a loose purple shirt that day, one that slightly fell off my right shoulder, plus a dark-blue bra and a pair of jean shorts. I remember knowing this would be the day, so I'd showered and shaved and scrubbed every bit of my body to perfection.

Pink Floyd's album *Wish You Were Here* was playing in the background. That became our song, and I cannot hear it to this day without thinking of Ponch. Although I was young – maybe too young – it was a great first time. We were safe, we used a condom, and a month or two later I would sneak to the doctor and secretly go on the pill without my mother knowing.

Following that experience there definitely was a new, quite different level of connection between us that hadn't been there before. That old adage, "I went into the room a girl and came out a woman," is probably true, but I just remember coming out feeling sore but happy – and also a bit worried that Ponch would now lose interest in me.

While things with Ponch were joyous and delightful, things at 'home' felt terrible. I was horribly angry at my mother for the situation she had put us in, and – despite my grandparents being really kind and loving people – I hated living in their home, sleeping on a twin bed in a room with my Mum-Mum. (My grandparents slept in separate rooms because of my grandfather's terrible snoring.) Her room was decorated in colors based on the inside of a 1983 McDonald's, and we shared an old white oak dresser where the drawers would stick like crazy when you tried to open or close them. (I mean, did they not have WD-40 in 1992?!)

This anger and frustration built and built. Then one day in late July, Ponch and I had had a wonderful time hanging out at the lake by his house, goofing and laughing with his friends. We ended up back in his big messy bedroom sitting in a circle while his friend Sean stuffed a bowl with pot. There were maybe six of us sitting in the circle. The bowl made its way around and I passed as I always did. I watched it make its way from person to person, and observed their facial expressions, the calmness and relief that touched the corners of their mouths, their eyes softening, shoulders relaxing and that slow release of satisfied smoky breath –

And I thought to myself: "Wow. They sure look like they're having fun. They look great – but all I do is feel like shit all the time."

I wanted that fun. I wanted to feel something – anything – different than what I'd been feeling at home ... all the anger and hopelessness.

As the bowl made its second pass and came into my hands, I paused and stared at it. I remember not really knowing how to hold it, though I'd now seen it done hundreds of times. And right then I decided I wanted the fun, the freedom. I wanted to feel calm and soft and relaxed. And so I hit the bowl.

I wasn't thinking about what time it was or what time Ponch's mom would be driving me home, or how I would react to smoking pot my first time. All I was thinking about was wanting to stop feeling so shitty. I wanted my whole, awful situation to just go away for a little bit. And well – it worked. Maybe it worked a little too well! Within moments of choking out the smoke, my eyes were watering but felt soft, my mouth started to turn up into a smile, my shoulders relaxed, and my arms felt like they weighed a hundred pounds.

And then came the laughter. Oh, the glorious, glorious laughter! Everything and everyone faded away around me, and all I could see, hear, taste, smell and touch was the laughter. I remember Ponch putting his forehead against my forehead and laughing with me, maybe *at* me, but at the time it felt like such a bonding moment.

At some point the rest of our friends left and it was just Ponch and me hanging out in his room. I felt so light and free, like I was floating in my own unique bubble of tranquility far and away from all the burdens of Richard and home and Mom … and I desperately didn't want to lose that magnificent feeling. Hey Mrs. Reagan, if this is my brain on drugs, then I'd like some more please.

After the necessary washing of hands, brushing of teeth, drops of Visine and practicing walking and talking like a not-high person, I was driven home and went straight to my room. I felt like a baby giraffe that had just fallen out of its mother – I didn't want anyone to know or see me on these unfamiliar 'stoned' legs. But I had new life in me now. I grabbed my diary and spontaneously wrote down a sentence that would define the next four years of my life. A sentence that expressed what I would chase after – day after day, year after year – that first delicious feeling of tranquility and release, that uncontrollable freedom and laughter.

"This is it. This is the answer."

And that was it for me – my first step on the way to becoming an addict.

IN RETROSPECT

Ponch was such an intense part of my youth and addiction. I look back now with no judgment on him, realizing that we were both just kids. I do not know where or how he is today, but I hope he is well. I'll never be able to hear *Wish You Were Here* without thinking of him.

It's amazing how clear that first moment of using drugs remains in my mind. And though – looking back – I don't know what I might say to myself at that age, I can at least now understand why I did it... I had the biological predisposition of addiction/alcoholism from my father, I was psychologically wrecked from my stepfather's abuse, and seriously down after being pulled from my home - AND I was hanging around with people who were regularly drinking and using. I just had too many strikes against me. Any one of those factors might have been enough of a trigger. But all three? I had no chance.

Now, as a healthy(ish) sober adult, I'd like to say something to 16-year-old Tracy: In the words of the movie *Good Will Hunting*, "It's not your fault." You were a child in a world of pain and confusion. Your next four years might be awful, traumatic, scary, depressing, exhausting, dangerous, humiliating, and all the rest – but you will make it through. Like a diamond forged with pressure and heat, slowly and surely you will come out shining.

|| Horse With No Name ||

Ponch and I broke up in December of 1992. It was awful – I was beyond heartbroken. A puddle on the floor, ugly-crying, destroyed. He had been my moments of joy and light in the storm of leaving Richard, fighting with my mom, living in my grandmother's room – all of the pain and reality I was trying so desperately to avoid.

In those months since we left our home in May, I had learned – for lack of a better term – that my soul was becoming filled with trash. What was in my trash can? I had my neglectful and uninvolved father – trash. I had the abusive words and fear of my stepfather swimming around in my head – trash. I had my overwhelming anger toward my mom for our current situation – trash. Despite loving my grandparents, I hated living in their home – trash. I wanted my posters, clothes, all the little things I loved, but they were in a cardboard box at O'Malley's Storage – trash. I was only 16 years old, and already so damaged. But I found that drinking (when I could) and smoking pot (as much and as often as possible) did this magical thing to my trash can. The drugs worked as a lid. A nice, tight, secure lid that kept the stench hidden away from my mind and heart.

Along with mourning the loss of Ponch, I was also consumed with a new realization – or rather fear – that I now had to find my own trash can lid. I had to establish my own dealer, connections, and paraphernalia ... fast.

Luckily, I had acquired some friends of my own while running around with Ponch, so I made a few calls and headed down to Wonderland in Philadelphia to assemble my own goodie bag.

I remember thinking, "Why didn't I do this sooner?" Not beholden to other peoples' purchases or schedules, it wasn't long before I was finding reasons to sneak out of my house to get high. I definitely felt a twang of guilt when I'd be stoned, watching a TV show with Mum-Mum. I'd be doused in Visine and breath mints, trying to make conversation and add inflection to my voice, when all I wanted to do was sit there and be comfortably numb.

And on the rare occasion when both my mom and grandparents were out for a period of time, I enjoyed sitting outside on the back deck off the living room. I'd bring my dog, Ruffles, outside with me, and we'd sit there together, happily relaxed and cuddling. I'd roll a joint and get high with Ruffles by my side. Ahhh. I can still see the view – it was quite lovely – though I didn't fully appreciate it at the time.

The living room had a wall of windows and a sliding door that led out to a long deck which looked out back to Pop-Pop's manicured lawn and below to the pool. Beyond the pool was a large, wooded area, open and private and beautiful. I would sit there, with my back against the windowed wall, feeling enjoyably high, doing nothing but petting Ruffles.

I would sometimes sing quietly to her. She was getting older and slowing down, but at the time I didn't give it much thought. I guess I was too wrapped up in my own empty life – my hollow family, my lacking an at-home functional father, my growing need to constantly be stoned, and overall teen despair.

There was one particular song I would sing to her over and over: *A Horse with No Name* by the band America. Ruffles, seeming to like the song, would put her fluffy white head on my lap and I would sing ... and in these brief private moments I temporarily felt satisfied. Ruffles loved me fully, and I loved her the same. Yes, I was a mess, I was almost always high, still living in my grandparents' home, remembering and struggling with all the demeaning words and hate that had too recently been spewed at me by my stepfather.

But for these brief moments I was somehow able to feel genuinely content with life, my trash can lid closed nice and tight and Ruffles by my side.

IN RETROSPECT

Recently I was watching a TV show with my younger daughter and *A Horse with No Name* was playing in the background of the program.

I said, "Oh. I used to sing this song to my dog Ruffles."

My daughter asked, "Really? Can you sing it for me?"

So I started to sing – but then I burst into tears. I'm crying now while I'm writing this. It's a cliché but some love really is forever. I want to go back and tell Ruffles how much she meant to me. She was a steady light in my storm. I'm so sorry I didn't hug her more when I had the chance.

|| Aerosmith + Peach Snapple = Zoloft ||

By early spring of 1993 I was a 17-year-old sophomore in high school and, because of my drug use, I had started to live two very different lives.

On the one hand, I had my school and girlfriends. I loved my small school, even in my worst times. I had wonderful, genuine, fun friends. We would laugh and tease each other at school, help each other study or finish homework on the fly. I grew to love the library, a place I could hide away to focus and get my work done before leaving school since I knew I would be useless after 4 p.m. Because I did well(ish) in school and was sociable, my girlfriends weren't concerned by the fact that I 'may occasionally smoke a joint on the weekends.' Little did they know, I was stoned daily just to feel like I could show up in life, my trash can lid secured.

On the other hand, I had my crew of druggy friends. The only 'fun' we had together was getting fucked up. There was nothing genuine about these people – we'd stab each other in the back if needed. I had established my dealers, paraphernalia, knew how to hide all the signs of drug use – and my ability to deceive and manipulate was getting better and better.

It was around this time that I learned the power of appearance. If I could just be cute, play the role of sweet private-school girl, do well enough not to turn heads, and seem to always be 'together,' people wouldn't notice that

I was actually falling apart inside. Especially around my mom and grandparents, I learned how to put on the perfect show. I would take full advantage of my mother's fine qualities of being kind, nurturing, generous and trusting. Though she did not work, it helped that she was distracted by my aging grandparents and managing her messy divorce from Richard, who wasn't physically present, yet was still so much a part of our lives.

Everything seemed to be colliding at once – my adolescence, a heightened focus on my body, the subtle internalized voice of my stepfather still continuing to put me down. This was compounded by my seriously sagging self-esteem as I increased both the frequency and types of drugs I was now using. Yeah, I could put on the show, but sadly there was so much darkness stirring beneath the surface of my façade.

So … I started to run. No, like, literally run. Running gave me a sense of control. I would put on my sneakers, grab my Walkman, pop in a cassette tape, and take off on a run. I would run up the street next to my grandparents' house to the local middle school where I would run laps around the track. I loved running laps – the mindless round-and-round repetition was oddly soothing.

I would just run and listen to songs like *Dr. Feelgood* by Motley Crue (relevant to my daily drug use), *Evenflow* by Pearl Jam (though I felt anything but 'even' during those days), and *Youth Gone Wild* by Skid Row (yep, sounds like me). My volume cranked to the max was definitely way too loud – I am now mostly deaf in my left ear – but it felt good. I started to look good too. Not only did *I* notice this change in my body, but my friends at school and drug buddies mentioned it also.

The running continued and I also started to add aerobics. I particularly loved the VHS series *The Firm* which incorporated weight training with aerobics and featured amazing 1980s spandex fashion and nut-hugger shorts. Watching myself in the mirror – curl, pull, squat, and lunge with weights – made me feel powerful. This was the only power that I currently had in my life. The only control I could exert at that time was over my own body. I couldn't control my dad not wanting to spend time with me, I couldn't control the nasty judgmental voices in my head left over from Richard, I couldn't control not living in my own home, I couldn't control my mom's indecision about where/when we should move, and I certainly couldn't control my daily need for drugs. But my body – that was mine to control.

And so I had a routine – often running in the morning before school, getting three, four, sometimes five miles in. Then I'd return home from school to do *The Firm, Volume 1* workout with Susan Harris and her canary-yellow leotard – did it so many times I knew every word she was going to say. I got to the point where I would pop in a cassette tape and turn off the volume on the video. I loved listening to Aerosmith's *Get a Grip* tape while I worked out. *Livin' on the Edge?* – You could say that ...

You might wonder – how could I run and exercise so much while coating my lungs in a thick blanket of pot tar and resin every day? Great question! In fact, I would have to stop every once in a while and hock up a black ball of phlegm from my lungs. I became excellent at spitting these sticky black and greenish loogies, launching them with impressive height and distance. Yeah, real yucky.

Towards the end of my sophomore year, I felt good. I thought I looked good. But then, as I started to wear less as the temperatures rose, Richard's attacking voice in my head got bigger: "You could lose some weight – your thighs are still a bit big – I don't think you should wear that, you look fat in it."

"Fuck you Richard," I'd react in my head. "I'm not done yet, I've got this."

And that's when I turned my attention to food. I would make a small adjustment. I simply decided to skip my Philly soft pretzel with cream cheese at school snack time. I sat with my peers at the table and chatted with them while they ate that delicious combination of salty carbs with cold cream cheese, squeezed in little dollops out of those individual-sized silver packets onto one bite of pretzel at a time.

Then I started to pack my own lunch so that I could control the items and portion size rather than risking it with whatever the cafeteria might be serving that day. I also learned how to count calories – probably the only math I was good at during my addiction.

Next, I moved my food focus to dinner. My grandmother was a truly phenomenal cook and would prepare great meals for the four of us – but I started to cook my own meals, using a measuring cup to portion out the exact maximum amount of angel-hair pasta and Classico Red Pepper Marinara sauce.

With Richard constantly berating me in my head about being fat, I literally half-starved myself. Quite quickly my daily limit of 1500 calories turned into 1200 calories, then 1100 and finally down to 900 calories per day. And just like with my drugs, I was excellent at hiding my extreme food discipline. I brought my lunch to school every day. I would take time preparing, distributing, and finally eating (picking at) my meals.

There would be rare occasions where I was particularly high - like, really, really high - and I would temporarily lose my control. I remember exactly what this looked like. "Hey, guys, can we go to Wawa and grab something to eat?" I'd say from the back seat of the car. There would be zero hesitation from the three guys I was often riding with, and I knew exactly what I was going to get – a Peach Snapple and Chocolate Junior Tastykake.

I still remember the overwhelming satisfaction of consuming those items while stoned. It was like my one time of release and comfort – after hitting the bottom of the bottle a couple times with my palm to mix it, I'd 'pop' open the Snapple and enjoy that first big sugary gulp. I'd then move on to the crinkly wrapper of the Tastykake – taking my time to lick off every last stuck piece of chocolate icing. Of course, I would then harshly punish myself for days after this loss of control ... but it was so worth it.

Soon my growing anorexic condition developed a voice of its own in my head. The voice wasn't Richard's anymore, or even mine for that matter. My anorexia now had its own interior voice – an encouraging voice that seemed to only want me to succeed:

"We've got this! If we can just get to that next level," it would say. "Just one more step. It's right there, you can reach it!" It would lie and lie to me. The voice was a lie. Control was a lie. And I kept sinking deeper into self-starvation mode.

One night in the Spring of 1994, after my mom caught me crying over my angel hair pasta and carefully measured Classico sauce, she confronted me about my eating and unhappiness. Thankfully I was too exhausted to fight with her, and she convinced me to seek help. She found a specialist in Philadelphia and I started seeing Dr. K, a psychiatrist, once a week to address my eating issues.

It was a relief to be honest with Dr. K about my eating. He was easy to talk to and a straight-shooter. He didn't give me any bullshit and I, too, was honest about my diet (but certainly not my drug and alcohol use). Between my addiction and anorexia, something had to give.

After starting the antidepressant Zoloft and working with Dr. K for only a couple of months, my relationship with food improved and I found myself relinquishing some of the control around my diet.

As I look back on that year of ever-increasing substances and seriously decreased food intake, I now wonder if the anorexia was a subconscious attempt of mine to divert my attention from my flourishing drug habit. Almost like my anorexia was a decoy problem so that I could continue without facing the real issue. Hummm. If so, that was brilliantly fucked up of me.

IN RETROSPECT

These days, for the most part, my anorexia bitch stays quiet. But I admit that sometimes she still whispers to me, pushing me to do just one more round in a workout, to skip just one meal in order to look 'extra' good for some upcoming event, and so on. Today I exercise for the love of fitness – mental and physical – and I am grateful to have a lifelong relationship with movement. In fact, I actually met my husband at the gym! (More on that later...) And most days I eat well simply because my body feels and functions better when I do.

All that said, I'm honestly not sure my anorexia voice will ever go away completely, and sometimes I need to use my own healthy voice to remind that bitch to shut the hell up!

***

My high school required us to do something in athletics every season. Because team sports would require me to stay after school, and that would cut into my using time, I just went to gym class. I was actually so 'good' at gym that I became the aerobics teacher for the other students. Looking back, I find this to be a funny juxtaposition. There I was, smoking pot on the way to and from school every day, internally crumbling, emotionally falling apart – but I'd still pop on those leg warmers, turn up the music, and teach a high energy-aerobics class to a bunch of private school girls. Yeah, life is weird.

|| Who Am I Dancing With? ||

We were all excited about the traditional Fall dance at school my junior year. My girlfriends and I decided to go together and not bring dates. My best friend at the time, Beth, was hosting a pre- and post-party at her house. We arrived at Beth's house that afternoon to help each other get ready for the dance – and to drink a couple of wine coolers. Since her parents were chaperoning, there would be limited wine coolers – so I brought backup alcohol for myself.

It was a lot of fun hanging out with my girlfriends. This was something I did less and less as I got more and more into drugs my last couple of years of high school. I didn't want them to know how far off the rails I'd actually gone. This progressive retreat from my girl gang was kind of a subconscious decision – I don't think I even knew at the time how bad things had gotten for me, I just knew I didn't want these school friends knowing the extent of my drug use.

So, while we drank a couple of wine coolers, I also took gulps of the vodka I had snuck to the party in a Sprite bottle. Alcohol would have to do since there were too many people around for me to try to sneak away and get high. This was not the best decision – but then again, I wasn't known for making good decisions during this phase of my life.

We all got dressed, popped a mint in our mouths so the dance chaperones wouldn't smell anything on our breaths, piled in a parent's car, and headed for the dance. I remember arriving at the dance, I remember dancing at the dance. But I don't remember any specifics – the decorations, who was there, who I talked to, what we did or said. The vodka and wine coolers had their intended effect.

But after the dance I do have a slight recollection of sitting on Beth's back-porch steps smoking a bowl at some point later that night. And then the next thing I knew I was waking up, pretty uncomfortable. I'd slept on the couch in her family room and woke up realizing I'd pissed the couch. Luckily, I was up before my friends so, as usual, I immediately went into cover-up mode, removing the couch cushions and cleaning them with soap and water. I had to then jump in the shower to rinse off and change my clothes – rushing through all of this while nursing a nasty hangover.

Dumb kid that I was, I thought I was in the clear. As everybody started to wake up, we talked about the night before while eating bagels and cereal. I chatted along, acting like I knew what they were talking about even though I didn't remember much. But then an hour later, when we were all packing our bags, Beth pulled me to the side.

She said, "Can I talk to you for a second?"

"Sure," I said. I wondered where we were going as she took me out back. Then she turned and held up my deep purple pouch. My goodie bag from Wonderland where I kept my pot, rolling papers, a bowl, and some other miscellaneous paraphernalia in this purple satin baggie. It tied at the top and was maybe 6x4 inches, just big enough to hold what I needed and small enough to conceal easily.

But now Beth was holding it. "My dad found this on the back porch this morning. I'm assuming it's yours," she said, quietly but directly.

"Oh ... Sorry about that." And I took it back from her hands.

"So. My Dad said to tell you that you're not allowed to drink at our house or bring drugs here again. Okay?" her eyes not meeting mine.

"Yep. I understand. Fair. Sorry if I got you in trouble or anything."

"I'm not in trouble – but don't do it again."

"No. I won't."

She walked up the stairs to the porch to go inside – but then turned around, looked at me and said: "Should I be worried?" There was genuine concern in her eyes.

"About what?" I replied casually with a slight laugh. Nothing to see here. Everything is fine. I've got this. Continue with your lovely day.

"Tracy, is it normal for people to carry around stuff like that?" She nodded towards the purple bag which I was now holding behind my back – out of sight, out of mind.

"Oh, this?" I briefly pulled the bag from behind my back, looked at it, shrugged, and hid it again. "This is no big deal; this is nothing. I just bring it out on special occasions."

"Oh – well, okay." And with that, Beth walked inside.

We never discussed it again.

At the end of the year, we were all so excited at school when we got our yearbooks. Everyone sat in the lounge on the couches or on the floor, backs up against the walls, flipping through page after page, screaming and laughing and pointing at the pictures.

I came to one page with photos of the Fall Dance that happened about seven months earlier. My eyes landed on one small picture showing the back of a girl's dress, the crisscross black-velvet straps. I saw her long blonde hair, wavy, hanging off to the side. The girl's head was kind of flopped over as she danced with some guy. Upon second glance, it looked more like he was holding her up.

I didn't know who he was. But I knew who she was.

Me.

Me bombed out of my mind.

IN RETROSPECT

I might mention that Beth's dad would become a huge supporter of mine throughout my recovery. I found out during recovery that his own father had struggled with alcoholism and addiction before getting sober. Her dad gave me his father's 20-year AA chip when I was maybe seven or eight years sober.

"You can't give this back to me," he said, "until you get to twenty years sober."

At that time, twenty years seemed absolutely insane, a lifetime in the future. But I'm now 27 years sober as I write this, and that 20-year coin that Beth's grandfather earned still stays in my makeup bag so that I see it all the time. I think about all the people who managed to get sober before me and the people who supported me in my sobriety along the way... like Beth and her dad.

|| Diagonal ||

Like I said, I didn't love drinking. Don't get me wrong, I did drink a lot – but I didn't love it. Marijuana worked much better for me as my secret self-medicating numbing agent. Alcohol usually didn't taste good, and it took a while to take effect. Then when it did take effect, I felt less in control of myself than on other drugs I enjoyed... plus I still stressed about all the extra calories.

Although beer tasted gross, it was usually the beverage we had the most access to as underage high-school students. And we drank whatever beer the person older than us could get, usually the cheapest option. The only reason to drink beer was to get drunk – but it made me feel stuffed and bloated. Why do that when I could just smoke a joint and feel great?

Hard alcohol was harder to come by at a party, but it definitely went down easier. I also knew I would get out of control on hard alcohol, so those would be nights I would have to find a way to convince my mom I was at a sleepover and not coming home till morning.

And then Zima came along, a malt beverage from Coors with the same alcohol content as beer, around 5%. It was like getting wasted on 7-UP. The bottles were cool, the beverage was yummy, and it didn't cause the bloating that beer did. But not all Zima stories are good stories ...

One warm Spring weekend day I was hanging out with my three fellow drug buddies: Mitch, Steve, and Adam. We'd been together all day, walking around the park, getting high, hanging out at friends' houses, playing video games (well, me watching *them* play video games) – a typical Saturday. But on this day Mitch and I got into a fight.

I should mention that Mitch was my on-again/off-again boyfriend throughout high school – he was a tangential friend of Ponch. Mitch was older, had a job, liked to party, and was pretty funny, though that humor often came with a temper. He was also a hot-headed driver – a stoned hot-headed driver – but he had access to good dealers and money, so... a girl had to make choices! I chose my addiction over my safety – mentally and physically.

And on what had been a beautiful, numb Saturday, he was recklessly driving my grandfather's big maroon Chrysler sedan around like an asshole. Pop-Pop had been nice enough to let me borrow his car for the day, so by the time we got to this big party I was on edge and livid with Mitch. Lucky for me, they had Zima – let the games begin! This was one of those wonderfully rare parties at a nice house with a deck and backyard. Best of all, the parents were away for the weekend, so the house was ours to enjoy. I ditched Mitch, thoroughly pissed off at him, and mingled with some other friends. The Zimas were flowing, joints were making the rounds, time was effortlessly flying by ... I was in my good place.

Then while sitting on a couch in the living room watching Pink Floyd's *The Wall* with some friends, I suddenly realized I was unbelievably fucked up – and very soon I'd need to be sober enough to drive home. Damnit. Being so hammered on alcohol felt totally different than just being pot-high. And I needed to somehow find a way to get my shit together and drive home. This was not ideal.

I got up, dizzy, and went into the kitchen to drink some water, eat some tortilla chips, and then fix my face in the bathroom mirror before leaving. I found my car, still feeling woozy, took some deep breaths and got ready to do the 25-minute drive home. I told myself I'd be okay. I wasn't going to be overly late – I could drive slow and just be really careful.

Unexpectedly Mitch came to the side of Pop-Pop's car and told me I shouldn't drive in my condition. The irony! I told him I had no choice, I had to get home or I'd end up in trouble. He glared at me – then just stepped back from the car and walked away. I started driving off down the road, every window down, trying to focus, trying to make everything in front of me stop blurring...

I remember looking in the rearview mirror at Mitch walking away. I remember stopping at the first stop sign, feeling a bit confused about where I was and which way to turn – and then turning right and driving off from the party.

Then, suddenly, I'm 10 years old again... and somewhere far away I hear myself say, *"Pop-Pop is picking me up today!?"*

When I was in elementary school, I would get so excited when Pop-Pop would pick me up from school. There was a road on my way home from school that had a big hill – big enough that if you went over it with enough speed you would 'get air' on the other side. My Pop-Pop had always been a very serious man – worked hard and ran a tight ship – so you can imagine my delight when he would make eye contact with me from the rearview mirror as we approached that thrilling hill. I would shout, "GO, Pop-Pop!" He would floor it, flying over that hill at top speed. We would slam down on the other side, my body flipping around in the back of the car, head bobbing, both of us laughing. We would arrive back at my house, and he would give me a little shake of his head, making sure I didn't tell my mom – it was our little secret.

The next thing I remember, my eyes were slowly fluttering open. The car radio was playing loudly. My seat was leaned way back. The car engine was running. As I slowly started to come into awareness, I realized that I was pulled over on the side of the road about half a mile from my grandparents' house. I had zero memory of arriving there or stopping the car. The last thing I could remember was making my first right turn – and then waking up here.

I looked at the clock and realized I would only be about twenty minutes late. Phew! But how did I get here? How long had I been asleep? I didn't know how any of this had happened. Confused but thankful, I straightened my car seat and got ready to finish the drive home – and it was then that I saw the top of the dashboard. Vomit everywhere! Oh my God.

I lost my momentary sense of relief and gratitude that I hadn't crashed into anything and started wondering what the hell had actually happened. And then the addict in me kicked in. Nothing to see here, I've got this, everything's fine, I'll just do my song and dance to make sure nobody finds out what had happened – just get it together, Tracy, stay cool. Get home, check in briefly with Mom and pretend to go to bed. No one was going to go out to the car when I got home. They'd already be in bed.

"Hi Mom, I'm home. Sorry I'm a little late," I said in a whisper after slowly opening her bedroom door.

She said, "Alright, honey. Are you okay?"

"Yes, of course. Mitch and I got into a fight, but it's fine. Whatever. I'll talk to him tomorrow – 'night."

"Aw I'm sorry, honey. Okay. Good night."

I closed her door and went into the bathroom to get ready for bed. After waiting for about 30 minutes to make sure Mom was asleep, I sneaked back into the garage and cleaned off the dashboard, making sure to be as thorough as possible, and then to hide the used paper towels under other stuff in the trash can by the side of the house.

"Safe!" I thought. I headed back to bed, exhausted.

A knocking on my door woke me up the next morning. It was my grandfather. "Tracy," he said evenly, "can you please come out here."

I got myself out of bed and opened the door. "Yeah, Pop-Pop? What's up?"

"Come with me please," he replied and started walking down the hallway. I followed him, my mind trying to think – had he found the paper towels? Did I miss something cleaning up? Did I leave something in the car? I had been so thorough and careful!

He opened the door to the garage and just stood there. It wasn't until I popped my head in the garage that I saw why he had brought me here.

Hummm. This was going to be hard to explain.

Despite my unbelievable attention to detail when cleaning up the prior night's vomit, leaving zero evidence of any bodily fluids behind, no paraphernalia on the passenger seat or weed seeds on the floor, somehow, I hadn't noticed my gross error – I had parked his car diagonally in the garage. Yup. I'd somehow managed to wedge the car in at an almost 45-degree angle without so much as touching a wall or pole.

Busted.

IN RETROSPECT

Along with many other choices of mine during that time, driving home drunk that night had been so incredibly stupid of me. I say this with experience, guilt, and fear: Never ever drive a car while under any influence – and – never get into a car with somebody under the influence. Ever. Hard Stop.

There is a little part of me that believes some magical force, like a giant invisible hand, had picked up my car and delivered me to that spot half a mile from my home. I'd like to believe the universe knew its plan for me, so it spared me (and others) that night.

And there is a funny postscript to this story. Months later, when the air had gotten cold outside, my grandfather had turned on the heat while driving his Chrysler one afternoon. I heard him talking to my grandmother in the kitchen. He was asking her questions about the last time she drove the car, anything she had noticed. And then I heard him say:

"It smells. I turned on the heater and the car stinks. Maybe something got into the engine – it smells like something is rotting, or like vomit."

Oops.

|| Always Sit Down ||

"Lessons in life will be repeated until they are learned."

~ Frank Sonnenberg

PART 1

99 Red Balloons isn't just a 1984 song by the German artist Nena. It also fairly adequately describes a Grateful Dead concert.

I liked the Grateful Dead ... I think. I don't even know if I *really* liked their music, but I definitely liked their concert scene – a bunch of people coming together peacefully and even joyfully who liked to get fucked up. That was a scene I could get behind. I could deal with the incredibly long and funky songs in order to be around a bunch of people with a bunch of drugs they wanted to share with me. Yes, *"I will get by, I will survive"* just fine. Mostly.

I had the opportunity to attend a number of Grateful Dead concerts, but one in particular stood out. I have absolutely no idea how I talked my mom into this, but I traveled with a group of drug-buddy friends to Washington DC in the summer of 1994. We had tickets to one of the shows at RFK stadium.

To be honest, going to the show was less important to me – it was the party happening outside the show where the fun was. This show was on a weekend, and we drove to

DC early on Saturday to tailgate before the night show. I'm sure the concert was good. (Weren't they all pretty much the same? I never could tell the difference between one Grateful Dead set list and the next.)

After spending most of the afternoon sitting on a blanket drinking and getting high, eventually falling asleep and having the sun burn my nose, cheeks, and arms, I entered the show pretty messed up. It was the same scene inside as outside, except that inside we had a live band versus cassette tapes.

After the show we somehow magically arrived safely at our shitty motel. Hey, a bed is a bed. A shower is a shower. I was eighteen. I didn't care about luxury, I cared about cost, and this was nice and cheap since half a dozen of us were staying in one room. Though the various smells and sounds that happened in the room that night were rather... displeasing.

After a not-awesome sleep, we all crammed into our friend Jim's truck and headed back to the RFK Stadium parking lot. The day proceeded as it had the day before. Lots of pot, shitty beer, listening to music, sitting on the blanket, dancing with strangers, eating junk food – then more pot, then *eating* pot, sitting around some more, having a few more beers ...

I remember everyone taking their shirts off, both boys and girls. I was wearing a loose colorful skirt, white shirt, and had a red bandana tied in my hair. So Bohemian! I joined in and took off my shirt, exposing my extremely-boring gray cotton bra. And at some point, I decided to go for a walk. Yeah, sure, that's fun – walking all by myself, lost in a giant tailgate party with thousands of Dead people, and me wearing a bra. Totally smart. Let's do that!

I came across a guy selling gigantic red balloons filled with nitrous oxide. I paid five bucks and was handed my big red balloon. Ahhhh. I sucked and sucked and sucked on my laughing gas.

Wahhhhh ----- Wahhhhh ----- Wahhhhh ------

Slooooooooooowly exhale.........

Things got fuzzy.

Suck suck suck suck suck.

Wahhhhh ----- Wahhhhh ----- Wahhhhh ------

Slooooooooooowly exhale.........

Things got fuzzier ...

At some point I felt a hand on my back. I was working on opening my eyelids. They were fighting me, like they were glued shut. I finally took a deep breath and started to come to in slow motion. My eyes lazily peeling open. To my left was an older man, probably in his 50s, maybe 60s. Worn-looking. Beard. Messy salt and pepper hair. He had his hand on my back and was also holding my left forearm.

I realized I was sitting on the edge of a curb with no idea how I got there – and this older man was kind of patting my back. I was still pinching my big red balloon, which had shrunk from me sucking on it. I finally made eye contact with the older man, and he unassumingly said to me, "You gotta sit down when you're doing those, little lady."

He smiled, nodded, got up and walked away. I just sat there and finished the balloon, sitting safely on the curb. Ah, that wise, wise old man.

PART 2

During Christmas break 1994, my boyfriend Mitch's parents went on a vacation. Jackpot. We got into a lot of trouble that week. Adam brought a nitrous tank to the party. He always found cool stuff, but he never disclosed his dealers or where he got us the nitrous, mushrooms or acid. He could be pretty annoying, but he got us drugs of all sorts, so we kept him around.

We were all hanging out in Mitch's living room watching *The Fugitive* with Harrison Ford. We'd had some alcohol and definitely pulled a bunch of bong hits. Now it was time for the nitrous balloons. Adam filled them up and passed them out. Everything got quiet as our brains basically shut down. I couldn't even hear the TV in the background.

I have no idea why I got up from the couch and walked out of the room. Hadn't I learned my lesson to SIT DOWN from the Grateful Dead show just six months prior? But – the next thing I knew, I was lying on my back in the hallway next to the stairs. I mean, flat out on my back. I started to open my eyes, but something seemed wrong with my right eye.

Whatever. I was extremely fucked up, and my brain was fried with nitrous, so I just kind of rolled over to my side and pushed myself up. I was still pinching the balloon in my left hand. Unbelievable.

I stumbled back into the living room – who knows how much time had passed – where Steve looked up at me and said, "JESUS!"

Everybody looked at me and started freaking out, but I had no idea what they were freaking out about. Mitch quickly hopped off the couch and came over to me. "Where did you go? What the fuck happened?"

I didn't know what the big deal was. I had simply walked out of the room, fallen down, and come back. Right? But as I was thinking that, Mitch reached his hand up to wipe my face – and when he pulled his fingers away, they were covered with blood. My blood.

I was led into the kitchen where Mitch wiped off my forehead with a wet paper towel. Oh, *that* was why my eye was weird – there was blood in it. Mitch cleaned up the cut, which was on the inside of my right eyebrow, and we tried to piece together what must have happened.

I pointed toward the hallway that led to the stairs.

"Shit, Tracy. Seriously – fuck." Mitch went and found the broken frame and glass from a picture of his family.

"Sorry, Mitch. I didn't mean to," I apologized.

I assume that (for some unknown reason) I had walked out of the living room and directly into the wall instead of turning to go up the stairs. My face must have hit the glass-framed picture hanging there, cutting my eyebrow. I don't know if I then passed out or was just stunned, but I fell backwards onto the floor and lay there for a period of time – enough time for the cut on my eyebrow to begin bleeding and dripping down the side of my nose and into my eye.

Dammit. That wise old guy at the Dead concert had been right – always sit down.

IN RETROSPECT

I still have a bald spot on the inside of my right eyebrow. I cannot seem to grow hair there and regularly fill the spot with a brow crayon. And while I don't anticipate sucking down any nitrous balloons in my future, my little bald spot reminds me that if I do find myself with a red balloon: Sit. The. Fuck. Down.

Public Service Announcement: In addition to eyebrows, nitrous balloons can totally destroy your brain and be incredibly dangerous. My half-brother had a friend who died from doing nitrous. The tank had been incorrectly hooked up and it froze his lungs. He couldn't take in a breath and he suffocated. That's beyond tragic... and scary.

|| These Pants Are NOT Flattering ||

Ok, where was I by this point? By now I'd been using (well, abusing) alcohol, pot, nitrous, mushrooms, acid, and a touch of cocaine. Anything to keep things stuffed down inside me – keep the lid on my trash can.

Today our feature program includes hugs and music and glow sticks and dancing and ridiculously baggy pants. You guessed it – ecstasy.

Eliza loved ecstasy. She was one of my few female friends who enjoyed drugs from time to time, and she was super into the whole ecstasy scene – the clubs, the clothes, the dancing. And let's face it, I was at the point in my addiction where everything was becoming a shrug of the shoulders and a "why not?" approach. Anything to keep the lid on the trash can and escape my daily reality.

So, when Eliza invited me to her house for Saturday night, I was excited – but also a little nervous. By that time, I had been exposed to a variety of drugs, but ecstasy hadn't been on the menu. That said, a night at one of Eliza's clubs seemed like an adventure I was open to.

When I arrived at her house wearing my usual – jeans and a concert T-shirt – she took one look at me, grabbed me by the hand, and dragged me up to her room.

The walls were covered in posters and knick-knacks, with clothes everywhere. It was overwhelming compared to my grandmother's bedroom, where there was none of my own stuff. No posters were allowed and all my knick-knacks were still in an (unlucky) four-leaf clover box at O'Malley Moving & Storage. As I stood enjoying her posters and decor, Eliza started tossing clothes out of her closet at me. After a few outfits, she finally got me looking the way she felt was appropriate for where we were heading that night.

When her mom called us downstairs for pizza, I awkwardly walked into the kitchen wearing my new 'going-out ready-for-ecstasy' outfit – insanely baggy, blue, parachute-leg pants, a rainbow belt, and a cut-off gray t-shirt with tiny capped shoulders. My hair was in some kind of braids-and-pigtails getup, and I had three chokers around my neck. I didn't look like myself, I didn't feel like myself. I felt somewhat ... ridiculous.

And – I was meeting Eliza's mom for the first time. "Hi, I'm Tracy! Eliza and I are friends at school. So nice to meet you! Thanks for having me over tonight." Blah, blah, blah. By now the addict in me had learned to be the first to speak to parents, employing a high-pitched cheerleader-sounding positive girly voice. Hand extended for a shake, eye-to-eye contact. *Nothing to see here, parent/adult, I'm not someone to worry about.* Smile, smile, smile.

"Sure, Tracy, hi," she replied. Didn't even look up. "Eliza, we will leave here in about 20 minutes. Can you two get a ride home?"

"Yup, Mom, on it," Eliza replied casually.

We grabbed some pizza and diet sodas (caffeine needed for a late night) and headed back to her room to finalize our makeup – so much eye-makeup that I think I must have looked like a clown.

"So, your mom is cool with us going to this club?" I ask Eliza.

"Yeah, she doesn't really care what I do. It's great."

Wow, I thought to myself. How much easier my life would be if nobody was paying attention to me. Keeping up the good-girl ruse was exhausting. It would be easier if the adults in my life didn't even make eye contact with me.

Her mom drove us to the club, which was about half an hour away. It was a silent, super-awkward car ride. I was really in my head, suddenly hyper-aware of what I was wearing and how 'not-me' it felt. And though I was curious and excited to try ecstasy, the fear of not knowing what to expect from it was scary. I knew pot. I knew my limit with alcohol. I knew how to plan to come down after a bit of coke. But here I was, wearing something I wouldn't normally wear, about to hang out with a group of people I'd never met, in a town I didn't know, with a casual friend who occasionally smoked pot with me before school in my car. Still, I was determined to do this even though it made me feel super nervous.

We got dropped off outside the club. I could hear the music pumping before we even opened the car door. I politely said goodbye to Eliza's mom, who again barely made eye contact with me. I tried to find my inner bearings – the pot I'd smoked before coming to Eliza's house had worn off.

Inside the rave it was wild: flashing lights, blasting techno music, and a crazy mass of human bodies moving all around us. A short guy with bleach-blond highlights waved Eliza and me over to the side of the big club building. She started hugging a variety of friends. I was introduced but didn't get into the hugs yet. And even though everyone around me was wearing almost the exact same thing as I was, I felt ridiculous. All I kept thinking to myself was, "Damn. These pants are not flattering on me. Not. At. All."

And then – just like that – I saw white pills in Eliza's hand. She passed one to me. Gulp. Here we go. Maybe I wouldn't feel as ridiculous once the ecstasy kicked in. Eliza's friends didn't look like or act like the group of people I'd spent the last few years partying and hanging out with, but they were nice to me. We tried to talk (loudly) over the electronic music about our schools and so forth. I watched as Eliza and some of her friends started dancing. Their moves were fantastic, even mesmerizing.

I slowly started to feel looser and less awkward. I found myself walking away from the safety of the mirrored wall behind me and joining them as they did their rave-dance moves – and it was fun! I didn't mind the looseness of the pants or the exposure of my midriff. My little braids were hitting me in the face from time to time and that was actually cute.

I don't think I even knew I was high. I just thought I was, well, dancing! It was odd how it snuck up on me – not at all like the obvious inner shift, the immediate transformation I would get after hitting a bowl really hard.

It wasn't like guzzling a beer followed by a shot of bourbon and knowing I'd soon start to feel the booze. Ecstasy was actually a bit like acid. You put those little tabs on your tongue, not really knowing how much they'd affect you – and then all of a sudden, they do. It took a bit to kick in ... and then it was a slow steady burn.

At some point I found myself sitting with my back against the club's big, mirrored wall again, chilling out and drinking a Sprite. After dancing non-stop I was insanely thirsty.

One of Eliza's friends sat down next to me. We chatted for a bit and then he asked, "Do you do meth?"

"No, I haven't done that," I calmly replied with a smile, feeling quite pleasant and comfortable at this point. Maybe it was late, I'd lost track of time, maybe the ecstasy was wearing off.

"Here," he said, and passed me a pill.

No thought. No real decision. Gulp. Down went the meth with the Sprite. I really didn't think anything of it. It could have been a Tylenol for all I cared. Drugs and alcohol definitely lower a person's inhibitions. You're much more likely to do or say things you wouldn't normally. You're simply not thinking clearly – and of course that was the whole point of doing drugs and alcohol in the first place. So here I was, popping meth. Something I probably wouldn't have done if I hadn't been high on ecstasy. And ecstasy was something I may not have done had I not spent a lot of time around pot and people using other drugs. It's a slippery slope...

I wasn't sure if it was because I was coming down off the ecstasy or what – but the meth was NOT a pleasant experience. I stayed immobile, leaning against that mirrored wall, my arms wrapped around my knees, internally freaking out. People were talking to me but all I could hear was the blood pumping in my ears and the roar of muffled music. I could see their lips moving but I couldn't really make out what they were saying. I would occasionally laugh or nod as a socially appropriate response to their possible comment. No, I wasn't hungry, I wasn't thirsty, I didn't want to dance – I just wanted to somehow make sure my eyes didn't pop out of my fucking skull.

I'd had bad trips before so I knew this would eventually pass, but in the moment my loss of control felt seriously distressing.

By the time we left the club with a friend of Eliza's who drove us home, I was starting to feel less weirdly amped. I was in an in-between coming-down state of itchy internal agitation while my mind and body also felt totally zapped. I was thankful to arrive back at Eliza's and get into a spare bed. I didn't take off my makeup or remove the braids from my hair, I just peeled off my tiny gray shirt and unflattering pants, put on some pajamas, and got into bed for a fitful sleep – glad to be away from the mirrored wall, the blasting music, the laser lights.

When I woke up the next morning it felt like someone had put my brain in the sun to dehydrate – I felt mentally fried and emotionally sunburned. Reduced. Shrunken. Diminished. Dumb. Sadder than sad. I was already living a dark life, but this was seriously low relative even to my usual low. And to make matters worse, I looked as bad as I felt. When I got up to use the bathroom, moving slowly with a different type of hangover than I'd felt before, I peered in the mirror and saw a crazy raccoon staring at me. My eye-makeup had smeared and my braided hair was sticking out in all directions – I looked like death by electrocution.

I got myself and my things ready to leave, moving slowly, like molasses. In the car on the drive home with my mom, I simply told her I was tired from a fun night of trying on lots of makeup and Eliza doing my hair. That wasn't a hard lie to sell given my disheveled appearance. Later that day I was able to get some time alone where I could get high, but I couldn't shake this heavy feeling, this emptiness that stuck with me from the previous nights' drug use. I didn't know if it was the ecstasy, the meth, or the combination – but they were both drugs I thankfully didn't use again. Besides, there were other drugs I would be trying soon enough...

IN RETROSPECT

After writing and re-living this story as a sober adult, I am baffled by my lack of discernment. Instead of pausing to think, "What the fuck did I do last night?" or "That was rather unsafe, crazy, irresponsible," I just made a mental note to not do ecstasy or meth again. It's clear that I was in deep, considering nothing wrong with this Saturday night scenario. Sadly, things would need to get much worse before I would start to see things with any clarity.

|| Road Rage ||

Mitch liked to drive fast. And it's not like he drove the type of car where one might be able to get away with this 'hot-rod' type of assholery. He drove a 2-door 1986 Honda Civic Si Hatchback – oh, in powder blue. Let that sexy image soak in for a moment.

As I mentioned earlier, he was often angry, and one night his road rage got particularly bad. We were stuck in a long line of traffic in a small hip town just outside of Philadelphia. It was a Friday night, so no surprise the town was hoppin'. Mitch was gunning forward, tailgating, honking, just being a real dick.

"Mitch, ease up, there is no way around this," I yelled at him. "Where do you want the cars in front of you to go? Fuckin' cool it!"

But then a car pulled right in front of us from a side-street – and Mitch lost it, riding his bumper, honking, yelling out the windows, giving the guy the finger. Finally, the guy put his car in park and got out. He casually walked back towards Mitch's car, to the passenger window where I was sitting. Mitch had already started yelling profanities at him as the guy crouched down and leaned in my open window. Then he raised up a pistol – and without uttering a word – pressed the cold, round tip of the barrel against the side of my head.

Mitch and I sat there frozen. Not breathing. The guy calmly looked at Mitch and said: "Would be a shame to mess up her pretty face. Do you think you could back the fuck off of my bumper?"

Silence. Time went by. I looked straight ahead – unblinking, unmoving. I thought maybe Mitch had passed out or something until, out of the corner of my eye, I saw him just slightly nod his head in response.

But the gun was still pressing against my right temple. It seemed like it was there for hours but it couldn't have been more than half a minute. Cars behind us started honking. Finally, I felt the pistol pull away from my skin. The guy stepped back from the window, concealed his gun, and slowly walked back to his car.

Mitch and I didn't say a word for quite some time as we drove on – and we never spoke about it again. But to this day I vividly remember what the round tip of that gun barrel felt like against my temple. The steel was cold and hard and heavy. Solid and unforgiving. Terrifying.

|| What a Long Strange Trip It's Been ||

I learned many of my addiction lessons after I got sober, but some – when I was lucky – I recognized quickly once the drugs or alcohol had left my system.

Take coke for instance. I only did it in small doses. I liked the rush and unique energy it provided – it was different than the usual numbness provided by marijuana. What I didn't like was being around cocaine people. They were often edgy, unpredictable, and angry – and those were feelings I was using drugs to *avoid*, not pay money for!

Or pills, mainly painkillers – I personally found them good, not great. Sure, they helped add to my blasé mood as an occasional 'topper' if they were present at a party. But I already struggled with constipation, so the pills just weren't worth it.

No heroin. Hard stop.

Crack? Keep reading... we'll get to that shortly.

Nitrous? Yes, please!

And then there was acid.

It was a beautiful summer day, 1994. Adam had scored our trio some good acid. Since I expected we would be tripping all day, I told my mom we were going to an amusement park – either Hershey Park or Six Flags Great

Adventure. A place within driving distance that required money for entrance and time to drive to and from. (There was always a solid cover story...)

I was excited to do acid again. I had done psychedelics a couple times up to this point, both acid and mushrooms, and I genuinely enjoyed my trips. But today was special. Since we had planned ahead, we would be doing two tabs of acid, up from our usual one.

Mitch picked me up that morning, and we met with Adam and Steve in the parking lot of a local diner. We hopped into Adam's car, and he pulled a little baggie with a small white sheet from his glove compartment. He then proceeded to use tweezers and scissors to carefully separate the little tabs. As Adam was separating them, he noticed he had two more tabs than he had purchased. (Dealers would do this sometimes to get in your good graces, ensuring you would return to them for product. They would also do this so you 'owed them one' in the future).

Adam looked at us and shrugged his shoulders. "Should we do them? I can cut them in half," Adam said with a smile.

It was rare, extremely rare, that I would hesitate when being offered additional drugs. But I did think to myself that we were already doing twice what we usually do, and now we were adding another half tab to the mix?

"I'm not so sure..." I confessed to the guys.

"Tracy, you don't have to be home for, like, 14 hours. It'll be fine," Mitch reminded me.

"Ok, I suppose... Ok." I was hesitant but decided to go along with the group and do the 2.5 tabs of acid.

Based on the day that followed, I can provide several lessons that may save you a lot of trouble in the future:

Do NOT take the additional half tab of acid. Even when it's free, even when your friends are doing it, even when you know you don't have to be home until 11pm. Do not do it!

Do not go somewhere public, like an arcade for example, when tripping your balls off on acid. It's highly terrifying, overwhelming, and upsetting. The lights, the sounds, the people. Too much.

Do not go for a walk in the woods. I can see why this might seem like a good idea at the time. You may feel like you have literally melted into and become one with nature, that you can feel the beating heart of the trees and the sound of the grass as it grows. That's lovely... until your eyes start to play tricks on you. That one little innocent bug you see walking on the log may turn into hundreds of bugs, and not just on the log but now they are all over you... and you will freak the fuck out!

Do not go anywhere without a set end point that you can see or know. (Please see "Do not go for a walk in the woods" above). Time and space are flexible, malleable, and complicated when tripping on a lot of acid. I remember that our walk in the woods seemed to be taking forever. Forever! I was exhausted and fearful that we were utterly lost in a strange forest. That's when Steve pointed behind us and confusingly said, "Isn't that our car?" We had walked about a hundred yards down the path and could still see the car in the parking lot of Valley Forge Park.

Do not look in the mirror. I had heard this from other people before, but I found myself drawn to look. Bad idea. My eyes looked like giant black saucers, the pupil completely covering the blue iris. My face moved, altered, contorted into funny things. I don't know how long I sat at that mirror, but at some point, we melted together, just like when the liquid mirror encases Neo in The Matrix. Things got dark.

So, reader, I'd like to take a moment to remind you of the original lesson: Do NOT take the additional 1/2 tab of acid.

|| Lunch Break ||

I'd arrive at school high pretty much every day. On time, prepared, engaged ... but high. As I mentioned, getting good grades was important for maintaining the ruse both at school and at home – I'm fine, no reason for concern here! All my time at school was spent in class, studying in a cubby in the library, or hanging out with friends in the class lounge. Or - when I became a Senior - driving to pick up my numbing agents.

After totaling my grandmother's blue Buick the year before, I had recently built enough trust with my Mom to warrant getting my own car. It was a shiny, new (well, used), bronze Honda Accord. And the freedom felt good.

The seniors at our school were allowed to leave campus for lunch or during breaks in their schedule. On days I knew I'd have lunch followed by a free period, I would have just enough time to leave school and speed down Lancaster Avenue to get to West Philadelphia.

There are many parts of West Philly that are beautiful. The University of Pennsylvania, for example, is in West Philadelphia, as are some adorable neighborhoods and excellent restaurants. But the strip of West Philly I would frequent wasn't as attractive – populated with run-down rowhomes, many of which were abandoned and frequented by vagrants. And that's where my dealer – Moses – was located.

Moses sold drugs out of a small corner-convenience store. It was painted white on the outside, the wood rotted and chipped in places. A red, green, and white sign hung out from the roof above: "7-UP." The store was small – just two aisles of snacks and household items. There was a bulletproof wall of glass towards the back of the store where you would pay by slipping money into a little open rectangle on the counter.

I would park my bronze Honda Accord wherever I could on the rutted street and then casually walk over to the little convenience store, my navy-blue kilt wrapped around my waist, white sneakers, blonde hair bouncing. Yeah – to put it lightly, I must have looked a bit out of place. Nonetheless, Moses and I had a good relationship. I bought a lot of pot, hash, mushrooms, and occasionally other goodies from him, which made him (and me) happy. On this particular sunny spring day I had to park my car across the street because things were busy.

Ding-a-ling, the bell above my head sounded as I pushed the door to enter the store. I walked right to the back and spoke through the bulletproof glass wall.

"Moses here? It's Tracy," I said to the guy sitting there.

"Yeah, what you want?" he asked in a monotone.

"Two." I'd done this often enough that I figured he knew what 'two' meant.

"Yeah, wait there."

He got up and walked into the back area which was covered with beads in the doorway. The beads were painted to show a picture of Bob Marley. Fitting. I walked to the front of the store and waited a few minutes for Moses to get my 'order' together – two ounces of pot, rolled up in two sandwich baggies. When Moses came sauntering toward me, I handed over the cash, turned my back on him and tucked the two baggies into each boob of my bra. Then Moses and I shook hands, smiled, and nodded to each other. I said, "See Ya," and left the store.

Nice! This was a good amount of pot – life was good. But as I jogged to the other side of the street, my foot stepping up on the curb, my car in sight, I heard somebody yell out: "HEY!"

I stopped and turned to see a cop standing on the other side of the street, just a few doors down from Moses' store. He was looking right at me. I froze. I didn't say anything, and I didn't move.

Again he shouted: "Hey! Can you come over here?"

My mind was racing a mile a minute. Oddly enough, it wasn't until that moment that I realized how obvious it all was. Me, a prissy-looking private school girl coming to buy drugs in a shady West Philly convenience store. It was like a spotlight was suddenly on me.

I didn't know how I was going to get out of this one, and I got really real with myself in that moment. I was fucked. So fucked that, as I quietly and slowly crossed back to the other side of the street, I readied myself to silently put my hands against the wall and be searched. I'd totally cooperate. That had to count for something, right?

As the cop slowly walked towards me on the sidewalk, I heard Moses exit the convenience store – the little ding-a-ling chime of the bell when the door was opened.

"Hey, my man! How you doin'?" Moses walked over to the cop and patted his shoulder.

The cop looked at him. The cop looked at me. The cop looked back to him. "Good, man. How are things?" he said to Moses.

"You know, just another day. Been busy this week with people out in this nice weather."

They were... chatting? Chatting! About the weather? I still stood there. Frozen. Ready to soon be frisked.

Moses looked directly at me, jerked his chin up, and said – "See ya."

The cop gave me an ever-so-subtle nod, a nod I might have missed if my senses weren't on such high alert at the moment.

And that was it. That was my cue to nod back, continue across the street, get in my new-ish bronze Honda, and drive back to my private school on the Main Line with my bra filled up with pot.

That was close.

But that wouldn't be my last close call.

|| Slippery Slope ||

Slippery Slope (*noun*)

- A tricky precarious situation, especially one that leads gradually but inexorably to disaster.

- A chain of events that, once initiated, cannot be halted; especially one in which the final outcome is undesirable or precarious.

Source: The American Heritage® Dictionary of the English Language, 5th Edition.

I genuinely believe no one sets out to be a drug addict. That would be ridiculous, right? Nobody tries a little something at a party - a wine cooler or beer or hit of pot or a mushroom or a pill - and is suddenly hit with the reality of what one's life will look like in 4 years after trying that one harmless little thing that everybody else is doing at the party. But the truth of the matter is that you have to start somewhere. As innocent and docile as that little something/somewhere might be, that very well could lead to something/somewhere entirely different. It is a slippery, slippery slope.

I had a hit of pot. I loved it. Then I had many more hits. And during the times that I was smoking and drinking, I was exposed to more and more drugs, watching people use these drugs successfully and with pleasure. I would eventually make little leaps in my brain to justify the next thing. To excuse it, to make it seem validated, even. Like a natural, harmless addition to the fun.

But what I didn't realize was that this was my disease talking. It was growing, progressing, rationalizing these decisions, casually talking me into the next bad decision ... all the while "Tracy" was shrinking. The person I had been – the silly, carefree, soft child – was disappearing. And replacing her was a disengaged, cold, selfish junkie.

Pot is natural, and resin and hash basically come from pot, so it's the same thing. I can do that.

Pot is natural, and mushrooms are natural. I can try that.

Mushrooms are a hallucinogen; I've easily handled that. Acid is a hallucinogen. I could try some acid.

My friend Eliza likes ecstasy and has no problem with it. I could try that with her. Her friends seem nice and safe, so I'm sure this meth her friend is handing me is also totally fine.

I've tried pills before, like ecstasy and meth. I can try this pill that my friend Rick's older brother is handing me. It's even a legally sold drug! It's not like I'm buying a whole bottle of painkillers to use on my own. I'm not that bad.

I'm not going to snort cocaine, that's insane. If you snort cocaine, you are obviously an addict! But if a little bit is sprinkled on top of this bong hit, that's okay. Let's be clear – I am NOT snorting cocaine! Smoking it? Hum. I smoke lots of things – I can justify that.

Ok, ok. I can do a little bump of cocaine on my hand. It's not like it's a whole line on a fucking mirror. I'm not snorting a whole line of cocaine like a drug addict. Not like 'that' guy – he's got it bad!

And so on, and so on...

On this particular evening, I drove down to the city to pick up an ounce of pot. An agitated guy I didn't recognize got into my car with little baggies containing white squares in them. It was crack. I didn't want the crack so I told him I wasn't here for that, and asked him to get out of my car – I was not interested. He said he would give it to me for a discount, just to try. Honestly, he was a bit pushy and making me a little nervous, so I gave him the 10 bucks and he gave me two small baggies and got out of my car.

I continued on to the next dealer to find the pot, which I purchased and started my drive home. It wasn't until I got to Mitch's apartment when I noticed the extra baggies of crack that had fallen on the car floor. The dealer must have mistakenly dropped them while pulling out a baggie for me.

I scooped up the extra baggies and walked up the flight of stairs to Mitch's small one-bedroom beige apartment. Steve was there, no surprise. They were attached at the hip.

"I got the pot. Here," I said as I tossed him the ounce. "And this creepy guy got in my car selling this other stuff. I didn't want it, but I bought a bag to get him out of the car. He dropped some more on the floor," and I dropped the four baggies of crack on the table.

Mitch was quiet as he looked at them.

"Dude, " Steve started, "These are crack rocks." We kind of all looked at each other until I shrugged my shoulders and said, "I know. Whatever. We don't have to do them. I just wanted the weirdo to get out of my car."

But we were all addicts, the three of us. And the little addict devils on our shoulders started whispering.

Excuse ... justification... rationalization... whisper, whisper, whisper. "You'll be fine, Tracy, you've got this. You're not as bad as those other people," my little devil tenderly comforted me.

None of us had done crack, and frankly I don't think we had ever actually been around it before. So we pretended to ignore the baggies and not even discuss them as we pulled tubes and watched TV. At some point later in the evening, as we were coming down off our highs, Mitch made a suggestion.

"What if we just put it on top of a bowl and smoked it?"

He didn't say the word 'crack' – that would make this too real. It was just ... IT. Yeah, if we just threw IT in with some pot, something harmless like pot, something we've done a million times, how bad could it be?

After no one protested, Mitch started to de-seed and de-stem some pot to pack a bowl. He then grabbed a baggie from the table and pulled out one little white crystal. He put it on top of the bowl and kind of smushed it in with his pinkie finger. He held the bowl to his mouth, angled it to the side, and flicked the lighter on.

Suck suck suck suck. HOLD.

As he was holding, he passed it to Steve. Steve hesitated for just a bit, his right knee bouncing up and down nervously, but he still hit it. As I watched Steve hit the bowl, I glanced at Mitch who was exhaling. His eyes were very wide. He gently shook his head, hands on his knees, back straight, eyes wide. He was smiling.

My eyes were darting back and forth between Mitch's reaction and Steve's inhaling.

Steve then passed me the bowl and lighter. My knee was not bouncing. I (stupidly) did not have any apprehension, and I didn't hesitate. Something in me clearly said YES.

Suck suck suck suck. HOLD.

I was used to the relaxed feeling pot gave me – feeling my muscles weaken and shoulders slump. I was used to everything softening and becoming less important or urgent. I always loved the role of 'numbing agent' that pot played in my life. But I was definitely NOT used to the bolt of lightning that I felt from smoking crack.

It was like that scene in *Get Him To The Greek* (2010 movie) when Russell Brand has to stab Jonah Hill in the chest with adrenaline after he freaks out from smoking a 'Jeffrey' (an absurd combination of almost every drug imaginable). Jonah Hill pops straight into the air and screams, "I'M ALIVE!" That was exactly how I felt. I didn't feel relaxed or soft, I felt energized and strong and awake! It felt different than my usual - better than my usual. I liked it. A lot. Like someone flipped on a light switch. Like I went into the phone booth Clark Kent and came out Superman.

We did "IT" again the next night, and same reaction - energized, excellent, awesome.... happy, even. Funny, strong... positive. After feeling so gray and bland for so many years, this UP feeling was welcomed!

A few days passed and all I thought about was having an opportunity to do IT (crack) again. I wanted to feel that rush and burst. And yet there was another voice that started to pipe up. This voice said, "Maybe this isn't a good idea. Maybe this is going too far. Maybe we are in too deep. Maybe."

Hearing this made me pause, wondering where that voice could have originated. But... I shook it off.

We had left the baggies at Mitch's apartment after using it those first couple of nights. I had said clearly to Mitch that he was NOT to do this by himself, and that he had to include us when we did it again. (I honestly didn't give a shit about "us" - what I really meant was "me.")

So when I marched up his apartment stairs that Thursday night, I knew we had two rocks remaining. We did our usual brief greetings and niceties before heading back to his room to begin setting the stage. Putting everything out on the little square side table, the paraphernalia, the little tools. All the things that made using drugs a relationship. Drawing it out, kind of like foreplay.

After the bowl was packed, he reached for the lighter. "Whoa," I said, "aren't you forgetting to add something to that?"

"Naw. That's gone," Mitch replied.

My heart sank.

"Gone?! What do you mean it's gone?" My voice was escalating.

"Steve and I finished that last night."

Silence.

Panic.

"WHAT?!" I screamed. I mean, I SCREAMED like I was possessed. I stood up out of my usual shitty cream-colored hammock chair from IKEA, marched over to where Mitch was sitting, and continued to scream in his face. "I was verrrrrrry fucking clear that you would not do that without us. What the fuck, Mitch?! You did both of them? BOTH of them!"

He stood up from his chair and started to yell back at me, but I shoved him back down. Hard! He looked shocked. I left the room, storming into the kitchen, walking toward the stairs, preparing to leave.

"Fuck you!" Mitch yelled at my back, then shoved me from behind. It caused me to trip over my own feet and fall on the floor. Being shoved, falling, and knowing the crack was gone – it all propelled me into a violent state of mind. I threw myself at Mitch trying to tackle him. Instead, he grabbed me and we wrestled. I got a good hit to his jaw with my right elbow, but as my body was still turned away from him in the follow-through, my back was exposed.

Putting all of his weight into it, he pushed me. The next thing I knew I was falling head over feet down the stairs. I remember hitting the closed door at the bottom of the stairs with a THUMP, all tangled up, arms and legs everywhere, hair hanging in my face. But within seconds I was back on my feet stomping up the stairs. The adrenaline pumping through me was unmatched.

When I got to the top of the stairs, Mitch just put his hands out in a "halt" position. I sincerely believe he hadn't meant for me to fall down the stairs, and I think it really scared him. I also think the fact that I popped up and stormed up the stairs preparing to continue our fight also scared him.

"STOP! STOP!" he started, eyes wide. "Jesus! I'm sorry! We were just fucking around - we didn't plan to finish it."

Breathing hard, my clothes and hair askew, I walked back into his bedroom, grabbed my bag, and left the apartment. I don't think we talked to each other for some time after that incident.

The next day at school, I was conscious of how hard the chairs and desks felt. I couldn't get comfortable. My hip hurt, my side hurt, my elbow hurt when I leaned on it. I hadn't realized it at the time, but that tumble down the stairs really did a number on me. How I wasn't more seriously injured was beyond me! But as I sat there in Dr

Warnett's history class, shifting constantly in my chair to get comfortable, taking the weight off my bruised hip or elbow, I had a moment of clarity.

You know the scene in the movie Jaws (1975) where Chief Brody is on the beach and sees everyone running out of the water because of the shark, and the camera zooms directly in on his face? Yeah, that's what I felt - like suddenly I was under a microscope. For the first time in a long time, I was seeing myself clearly. For just a moment I could see my addiction. I had possessed a decent amount of control up till this point, but I knew – I KNEW – that this little white crack rock was going to take me out. I knew it would cause me to lose the control (I thought) I had and be the death of me.

I don't know if it was the universe or a spirit guardian or my soul that spoke to me that day in class, but I never did crack again.

I will be 100% candid here – crack was both the best and scariest drug I have ever done.

Never, EVER do it.

IN RETROSPECT

This experience from beginning to end was incredibly stupid of me. Like, incredibly stupid. But I didn't think this was stupid at the time – this was a means to an end. A justification upon justification. A house of cards that started with one small, simple decision to not pass the bowl to the next person.

It's a slippery slope.

|| The Infection ||

It was early June, 1995. I would be finishing finals and graduating from high school the following weekend. My unhealthy on-and-off relationship with Mitch was nearing its end. Our mutual connections to dealers and party invitations would be the primary loss for me after we split up.

One night Mitch and I were leaving a party and he was pissed at me. I had won a bet on an NBA basketball game – it was something I had taken interest in, and I was getting quite good at betting on the winners. I thought Mitch and I had a friendly wager going that night at the party – until I won. As he was driving me back to my house he was yelling and saying he was not going to pay me the 20 bucks we had bet. $20 was a big deal to me, almost the price of a quarter bag – he was going to pay up!

As you can imagine, finding money – keeping money – was hard for a drug addict. I had made money throughout my addiction by working in restaurants as a hostess or food runner and doing odd jobs around the house for my grandfather, who was really aging by this point. I also traded the 'fake' money we used in the school cafeteria with friends for real money. And yeah, I often stole a $5 or $10 bill out of my mom's or grandparents' wallets – just a little here and there so they wouldn't notice. But most of the time, I stole little bits from other addicts or used my looks to get free dope.

As usual I was pretty fucked up leaving this party – no surprise there. I'd had some drinks and pulled quite a few bong hits. We weren't far from my house, maybe a half-mile or so, when Mitch said something about our bet that really pissed me off.

"Stop the car," I said.

He did nothing.

"I said stop the car. NOW! I'm getting out."

"No, you're not, you're being ridiculous – what do you know, idiot?" Mitch growled.

His comment triggered something in me. That *'what do you know, idiot?'* comment. I had heard that before, my stepfather's voice suddenly filling my head. This was something typical that he would yell at me: "What do you know, kid? You don't know anything. You'll never know anything."

I was hit with an overwhelming urge to immediately remove myself from Mitch's toxic presence. As he slowed the car to go around a bend, I opened my car door and just jumped out. I wasn't thinking at that moment, I was propelled by adrenaline. I hit the ground, rolled, and immediately pushed myself up onto my feet and started to run between two houses. I heard Mitch's car screech to a halt and then I heard him yelling my name.

"TRACY! TRACY! Are you fucking kidding me? Come back here!"

But I kept on running into the night – and then realized that I was more hobbling than running. My left foot was hurting with every step, but I was still able to put pressure on it so it couldn't be that bad. I was in my neighborhood and didn't have far to go. Soon I stopped hearing Mitch yelling, either because he drove away or I got far enough away – or I mentally blocked him out. I was just hoping he wasn't going to show up at my house.

I got close to the house and stopped, sitting in the bushes for a period of time, waiting to see if he would pull into the driveway. And it was while I was waiting in the bushes that I realized – shit – my left foot really hurt. I reached down to touch it and it felt bumpy. It was dark so I couldn't really see the details, but it didn't feel right.

When I felt the coast was clear, I snuck in the back door to my house which I had left unlocked. I turned on the light and saw that the side and top of my left foot was pretty scratched up and filled with pieces of gravel. Luckily the rest of me was pretty much intact. The palms of my hands were scratched up a bit and my left elbow was bleeding, but I would live. My jump out of the car had been successful – maybe even graceful.

I went upstairs (hobbled upstairs) and got into the shower. JESUS that really stung! I washed my foot as best I could before putting on a pair of socks and changing into pajamas. I then went downstairs and did my best to have some conversation with my grandparents and mom before going to bed. (The key was to give just enough to sound like you're not hiding anything, but not too much so they start to question your story.)

"Anyone watch the basketball game tonight?" I started.

"No, honey. Did you? Who won?" Mum-Mum asked.

"Rockets. They're going to the finals. Sam's dad is excited! He was fun to watch the game with, he was so into it." I made sure to mention parents being present at the party. All good, nothing to worry about...

Not sure my mom was buying it, but she wasn't saying anything.

Pop-Pop asked, "Tracy, could you please help me move the porch furniture out to the deck tomorrow? Now that the weather is getting nicer, I'd like to sit outside."

"Sure, Pop-Pop." But I was already wondering how to get out of it, feeling more concerned about my foot.

After suffering through maybe fifteen minutes of chit-chat and a rerun of The Lawrence Welk Show on PBS, I excused myself and went to bed.

My foot really hurt the next morning and looked a little swollen. Whatever. I was sure it would be fine. I went on with my Sunday – slowly and painfully carrying porch furniture to the back deck, sneaking out to get high, studying for my final exams, grateful for no word from Mitch, and finally going to bed. The next morning, I stuffed my injured foot into a sneaker and headed off to school. The following day I did the same thing. But by the third day it had become harder to ignore the swelling, the redness, and the smelly ooze coming from the side of my left foot. Finally, I knew what had to happen.

I found my mom doing dishes in the kitchen.

"Mom ... I had an accident a couple days ago and I have a scratch that doesn't seem to be getting any better."

"What do you mean you had an accident?" She turned around, flipped the dish cloth over her shoulder, crossed her arms and looked at me.

For some reason, I decided to be (mostly) honest. This was unusual for me. Maybe, deep down, I knew this foot thing was bad. Maybe I wanted her to take pity on me and my fight with Mitch. Either way, I quickly let it all ramble out.

"Mitch was angry at me because I beat him in a bet on a basketball game and when we were driving home he said some really mean things because he was angry that I won – things that made me really upset, and I don't know why I did it, and I know it wasn't a good idea, but I did ask him to stop the car - I asked him twice! - but he didn't stop so I decide to open the door and jump out."

She stared at me. Silent. Arms still crossed.

"And now my foot really hurts – see?" I pulled off my sock and lifted my foot up to the kitchen counter for her to look at. Her eyes widened and she inhaled an audible gasp. With the tip of a finger, she pressed around the edges, which were puffy and red.

"Ouch!" I said.

"When did this happen?" she asked.

"Saturday night."

"Saturday night!? What have you done with your foot since then?"

"Nothing." I replied. "I washed it off Saturday night, tried to clean it, and thought it would just get better, but it's not getting better. That's why I'm telling you, because I need your help. Are you going to help me or not?!" Suddenly I was making it her fault. Yeah, she was the asshole here.

"Well, this doesn't look good," she mumbled. "It looks badly infected. I think we have to go to the hospital."

"Hospital!? Can't we just put something on it and see how it goes?" I whined.

"No – I want someone else to look at it." She replied.

We drove to the hospital emergency room, and eventually I was seen by a doctor who told me the infection was quite bad. I was immediately hooked up to an IV antibiotics bag. They said I was lucky I came in then because if it had gotten worse, I might have lost my left foot.

In my hospital bed I watched my favorite basketball team, the Orlando Magic, lose Game One of the NBA Finals to the Houston Rockets. Shit – I never got that $20 from Mitch.

I was released from the hospital late that night, departing on a pair of crutches and with a prescription for antibiotics. I was told to keep the wound clean and uncovered – they probably also communicated the recommendation that I no longer jump out of moving vehicles. I was grateful to see the swelling and redness decrease over the next few days. By Monday I wasn't perfect, but I was able to stuff my still-swollen foot into a pair of white heels for my high-school graduation ceremony. Thankfully I was wearing a long white dress which hid my injury. I ditched the crutches and proudly walked down the aisle to get my high-school diploma.

It was actually a most beautiful day. My mom and grandparents were there. Even my dad showed up for the occasion. He gave me a ruby bracelet. Looking back, I remember thinking it may have been the most thoughtful thing he had ever done for me up to this point. In all my graduation pictures I'm smiling with my family and friends – smiling at finally finishing high school and being able to go off and away to college. Smiling through the pain of the infection in my left foot.

But my other 'infection' was bigger than just my foot infection – I actually had much more wrong with me. My negative attitude, reckless teenager behavior, selfishness, and addiction – it was all the predictable, almost inevitable result of being infected by a neglectful, absent, alcoholic father, a narcissistic, abusive stepfather, and any number of other shitty things I've mentioned. But still, it was me - I was an infection in my family system. As Taylor Swift sings: "It's me. Hi. I'm the problem, it's me."

IN RETROSPECT

I hated watching The Lawrence Welk Show with my grandparents – the performers dressed weird and the music sucked; it was so old and cheesy. And yet I'd give anything right now to sit between my Mum-Mum and

Pop-Pop on their couch and once again feel their unconditional love for me.

|| Tequila ||

Doesn't everybody have a tequila story? Mine happened during the summer of 1995 after my senior year of high school, just before I would be leaving for college. My cousin was getting married a few hours away, near the University where he and his fiancée met. My uncle had arranged for a luxury bus to take a group of the local family members to the hotel where we would all be staying. I was going to be on a bus for three hours with my extended family, followed by staying in a hotel room with my mom for two nights ... I was going to have to be a fucking ninja to somehow be able to sneak off and get high this weekend.

By this point, my mom suspected that something was off with me. The problem was, because of my relatively good grades, school attendance, and generally staying out of trouble, she had nothing concrete she could point to. In her eyes, maybe I was just a typical bratty teenager – my bitchiness wouldn't be surprising given the chaos of the last few years of our lives. Besides, she had been well-trained to wear those rose-colored glasses, which I knew how to exploit. And since we would be rooming together for the next 48 hours, I sure hoped she remembered to pack those glasses…

Before we left home, after a couple of hours answering my mom's ongoing question, *"What are you gonna wear?"* we agreed on the various outfits I would bring for the weekend. I packed my bag, chose some cassette tapes to bring, and preloaded two bowls that would be ready to hit when I found the right time to sneak away. Then we got on the bus. I was practicing tolerance, but my nerves were sapped and the nonstop chattering of relatives all around me was almost more than my teenage brain could handle.

The rehearsal dinner that night went fine, and on Saturday morning I was able to 'go for a run' before the wedding, giving me adequate time to get high. I remember the elastic waistband of my leggings being filled with the bowl wrapped in toilet paper, plus a tiny bottle of Visine, a pack of mint Lifesavers, and a bar of hotel soap to rub on my fingers to hide the smell.

I'm sure the ceremony was lovely, what little I can remember of it. The reception following the wedding was when things began to pick up. As the evening got going, I casually walked over to the bar area where a couple of groomsmen were standing and chatting. I smiled, blinked my eyes, and asked them to order me a shot. I took the shot off the counter, gulped, smiled, and said, "Number 2?"

Lather, rinse, repeat.

The next thing I remember, I was flying high and talking to a friend of the family. He was about my age, and I'd known him for years. He had always been a goody two-shoes in my eyes – never stepping out of line, always getting top grades, certainly never taking drugs or even swearing. That night his righteousness bothered me, and, being the asshole I was, I found myself provoking him.

"Just say one bad word. I dare you. Come on, just say 'fuck.'"

He looked at me and shook his head, with his chin down and his hands in his pockets. I was seriously drunk on tequila at that point, and I continued to verbally harass him – until l was interrupted by his dad who had been standing behind us listening to my mockery.

"Tracy, I think maybe you should go up to your room now," his dad said soberly to me.

Wow – that was embarrassing. Without saying a word, I walked away. And that was when things got a little fuzzy. I thought I actually *did* go back to my room. I don't remember anything past that embarrassing moment at the reception bar. The next thing I knew, I was waking up in my hotel room – experiencing a hangover of a magnitude I had never felt before.

But... according to some chatter among family members, I would learn that rather than going up to my room, I'd gone back to the bar and was drinking tequila, dancing with groomsmen and who-knows-what-else. I have no idea what had happened that night – and I didn't care at the time. What I did care about was how I was going to survive the next two minutes feeling as awful as I did.

It was time to start the long trip home. Oh God, the bus. I stared at that bus, dreading the endless journey ahead to get home. I would have to sit on that bus with my family members, knowing the gossip that was likely happening, having no memory of what actually happened, and the laser eyes of my mom staring at me with distain.

As we sat on the bus, my mom quietly said to me, "You are going to sit in this seat next to me, and not say a word."

"But what if I have to go to the bathroom? What if I get sick?" I asked.

"You better figure it out because you are not going to move a muscle or make a sound." Like a ventriloquist, my mom somehow managed to say these words through her clenched teeth as she smiled to others boarding the bus.

Shit. There was no way I was getting through this bus ride without vomiting. I started to panic, I started to think, I started to look around. My eyes landed on something in the trash can in the front of the bus. I slowly got out of the seat, walked forward, grabbed it, and walked back to my seat.

To this day I cannot look at a Smartfood popcorn bag without thinking of it filled with vomit. Thank goodness it had that opaque black exterior, hiding the insides. Thank goodness it was a large bag and not one of those snack-size ones. I just wish that crinkling sound of the aluminum had been quieter. Every time I needed to throw up in that bag I would open it, barf as quietly as possible, and then have to pinch the top closed to keep the smell and contents inside. I squeezed that bag shut for three hours, riding home with my head leaning against the seat in front of me.

And ... I never drank tequila again.

IN RETROSPECT

I really do like these cousins - they are truly good people. So, if they are reading this, I want to say that I really am sorry if I caused any disruption at your wedding. My bad.

ACT FOUR

~~~~~~~~~~~~~~~~~

Wild Thing

|| College Wishlist ||

Much like an animal adapting to its surroundings for survival, my addiction made it its job to be fed. Drugs and alcohol had once been 'nice to have' – they were fun for a period of time! (Not all my drug stories have bad endings.) But by my senior year in high school, I was on a daily 'need to have' basis. My survival instincts kicked in and I became skilled at finding the other addicts in the room.

It was like a Jedi mind power – I could be at a party and look around using my years of addict intuition and spidey-senses to figure out who was carrying drugs, who was high, who was up to take it to the next level. Yes, those were my people.

When I arrived at the University of South Carolina in late August, 1995, things were no different. Actually, I take that back – the difference was that there was an urgency. I needed to establish a dealer and a crew ASAP. I was in a new place with no drug connections or user peers. Luckily, since I had chosen to attend a huge co-ed party school, I assumed this shouldn't take long.

I spent my first night on campus alone in my dorm room while my mom spent the night at a local hotel. We had planned for me to also sleep at the hotel, but I let her know that I wanted time to set up my room so she could be surprised when she saw it the next day. This was partly true – I had become a bit obsessive compulsive since the sudden move from my home back in May, 1992. Controlling the environment around me, keeping my room organized and clean, knowing where everything was... These things became very important to me and gave me a sense of control – even though I knew, based on traumatic experience, that everything could change in a moment.

After my mom left for her hotel, I hustled to get my room set up and in order. This would then give me time to go poke around the dorm and campus. I started by walking around the floor of my dorm and introducing myself to the other girls. As I said before, a smile, handshake and good eye contact goes a long way toward building trust.

Eventually I came across Casandra, Cass for short, who was on my floor. She was a really pretty girl with wavy long dark hair – kind of quiet but poised. She asked what brought me to USC.

"Well," I started, "I'm from the Philadelphia area, but absolutely fell in love with this campus! It's beautiful and the weather's great. I also went to an all-girls school so, as silly as this sounds, it'll be great to have boys on campus." I smiled. "I'm also looking forward to the football tailgate parties that I've heard so much about. Go Cocks!" Giggle, giggle. [Note: The mascot for USC is the Gamecock].

I asked Cass about her coming to USC, and she said her older brother was already here. "We're from Virginia, so closer than you. With my brother being here, it was an easy decision."

Perfect, I thought to myself. Older brother. "Um, this is kind of direct," I say to her, "do you think your brother might help us get something to ring in the school year?" I say, this with my eyebrows raised and an innocent smile.

"Sure, I guess. We could go ask."

Yes... LET'S.

So Cass and I walked over to Sig Ep – Sigma Phi Epsilon – his fraternity. This was getting better and better! The Greek culture was a big deal at USC, and honestly this fraternity didn't seem so bad. The place wasn't disgusting and the guys seemed nice enough. But of course, just like me, appearances can be deceiving.

Her brother Chris laughed at my humble freshman request but gave us a small bottle of "grain alcohol" – Everclear was the name. I'd never tried grain alcohol before, and Chris did warn us that a little would go a long way. He was correct, and Cass and I had considerably more than a little that night in the dorm together.

Showing up for brunch the next morning with my mom was painful. I had to greet her at my dorm, cheery and bright-eyed to show off my prepared room.

We walked to get brunch at a small local restaurant. Sitting at an outdoor table with the sun beating down on my face, I had to pretend that every whiff of our food was not assaulting my post-vomit senses.

I don't know how I made it through that meal, but finally my mom drove off for home and left me – all alone. Alone!

No adult supervision. This was something my addiction had been longing for since the summer of 1992.

It wasn't long after she left that I was vomiting up my brunch in peace in my dorm bathroom. As I was leaning over the sink rinsing my mouth out, probably looking like death, I heard a raspy voice behind me:

"Nice way to start the journey! Care to share?"

I turned around to see a girl, short with thick, long, blonde hair. She wore an untucked Grateful Dead shirt and loose jeans with flip flops.

Our eyes met, and my spidey-senses tingled. Oh yeah. This would be one of my people.

Here we go.

‖ Musical Rooms ‖

Ashley and I became quick friends. Thick as thieves. We also had a unique situation. My assigned roommate, whose name completely escapes me because I maybe spent ten total minutes with her, had a dorm room but only to appease her parents. She planned to spend every minute at her boyfriend's place. And Ashley's roommate, Amy, was in the same situation. Her boyfriend Charlie had followed her to South Carolina, landing a job and apartment quite nearby. She used the dorm room to hide the fact she was living with Charlie off-campus. They were fun and loved to party – we liked them.

About two weeks into school, Ashley and I got to the point where we spent so much time together, it just made sense for me to pretty much move into her dorm room. Besides, her room was cooler – the bean bag chair, the psychedelic tapestries and Ashley's crazy art shit made the room feel rather homey. And we were very successful at finding good connections. Ashley and I worked networks on campus – Sigma Phi Epsilon being a big one (thanks, Cass). And Amy and Charlie found connections off campus. Things were looking up.

Ashley and I were two drugged and drunk peas in a pod. We could read each other perfectly – I never had to pretend with Ashley regarding my drug hungers of the moment – and really, we had so much fun together doing so many drugs.

There were a lot of students on campus who just smoked and drank on weekends and that was enough for them – but I was entirely of a different species. I hated, I abhorred, I simply couldn't stand *not* being high. I never got seriously physically addicted to heroin or cocaine or meth or whatever, but it was almost the same for me with pot and alcohol and psychedelics – I'd really freak out if I couldn't get high. Given the few previous painful years, I didn't do well with feelings or reality. Staying as removed and numb as possible was my top priority.

Ashley and I did mushrooms and acid a lot. They became our drugs of choice, along with my daily regimen of pot. Pot was my morning cup of coffee – wake up, smoke a bowl, shift into that altered state to avoid normal existence, then carry on through the day and night with several more rounds of smoke. And yes, it somehow all worked – no busts, adequate grades (in high school), playing the game, and doing just enough to get by. I was in college simply because it was the next thing to do – and I was going to enjoy every moment.

|| Peanut Butter & Jelly Sandwiches ||

One of my absolute favorite things to do late nights when I was stoned was to go to the student-center cafeteria and get cheese grits with syrup (don't judge this combo until you try it!). I would order a bowl of cheese grits, something I had never eaten before coming South, and pour syrup on top. The warmth and saltiness of the cheese and grits, mixed with the cool, sugary syrup – delicious. Ashley and I would sit around at a table with Amy, Charlie, Gavin and Doug, probably obnoxiously loud.

Gavin was a boy I was hooking up with here and there. He was cute and sweet, and I would be taking advantage of that. And Doug was a great drug connection. He and I would often butt heads, but we knew we needed each other. Ashley and Doug would end up getting together a couple months into school – and I hated this because she was way too good for him.

Another of my favorite things from the cafeteria were the peanut butter and jelly sandwiches. They were quick, easy, adequately filling – and cheap. I needed to save my pocket money for drugs and alcohol, not waste it on food. I would often bring a couple of peanut butter and jelly sandwiches back to the dorm room for us to eat before going to bed at night.

There was one particular week where Ashley was having a hard time – I don't remember why; all we did was consume and recover. That Friday morning, I got a call from one of my dealers letting me know he had scored something special and asked to connect with me around lunchtime in the cafeteria for the exchange. Nice! And perfect timing – weekend coming up.

I went to the ATM by the cafeteria and withdrew some cash, noticing how diminished my account had become. I would have to start figuring out ways to get (or save) money. I couldn't ask my mom to add another $100 or $200 to my account; I was going through money too quickly as it was. No way I was eating *that* much pizza! She might question me. Or worse, not fund me!

When I met with the dealer at an outdoor table, he handed me a decent-sized bag of mushrooms. I loved mushrooms! The taste was disgusting, but the trip was always unique and usually smooth. Acid trips could go downhill quickly – there was less control on acid, if that even makes sense. With mushrooms I could usually guide the journey a bit.

Before I left the cafeteria, I had a moment of inspiration. I got in line and ordered two peanut butter and jelly sandwiches. There was a little *"Walkin' on Sunshine"* spring in my step as I headed back to our dorm, excited to carry out my plans. Ashley had been a bit down for a couple days and I wanted to be her best friend and offer the 'shrooms to boost her spirit.

Once in the room, I grabbed the scissors on Ashley's desk and plopped down on the bed. I found her white and green cushioned lap tray that we used for our drug-prep and poured the bag in the center, separating the mushrooms into piles. It would be the perfect amount to split between the four of us – myself, Ashley, Doug and Gavin. Then, in the hope of lessening the yukky taste of the 'shrooms, I cut up two piles and put them into the two peanut and jelly sandwiches for Ashley and myself.

Ashley arrived an hour later. I sat with her out on our little patio while she smoked cigarette after cigarette, going on and on about her classes, teachers, a paper due, annoying students. I wasn't really listening – all I could think of were the glorious-mushroom-filled-peanut-butter-and-jelly-sandwiches awaiting us.

Ashley finally looked at me and took a breath.

"Sounds like you've had a long day," I said. "I brought you a sandwich." I hoped my voice didn't sound too desperate.

"Thanks," Ashley replied, kind of questioningly.

I went into our mini-kitchen and retrieved our treats – I was well past ready to get this party started.

"What is this?!" she asked after her first bite.

Busy chewing on my own first bite, I squeezed out a muffled reply: "Oh. Mushrooms."

"You got me a peanut butter and jelly sandwich and filled it with mushrooms?" Her smile widened as she grabbed her sandwich, stuffed a huge bite in her mouth, and said with her mouth full, "Best idea ever!"

I agreed, but truthfully it still tasted gross. Nonetheless, we persisted.

It was now after 7:00p.m. and we still weren't feeling the effects of the mushrooms yet, so we went to take showers and get ready for the night. We got into stalls next to each other and continued to chat, planning the night with Doug and Gavin. Then at some point we stopped talking and fell silent for quite a while.

It wasn't until a girl on our floor came in and said "Are you guys still in there? What are you even doing?" that we popped out of our mutual shower trance. I looked down at my waterproof Timex Expedition Indiglo watch. Holy shit! It was 9:00p.m. Ashley popped her head out of her shower stall the same time I did. Our glassy eyes met and we started convulsing with the giggles. Everything was impossibly funny. Mushrooms tend to do that and it's a delight.

We returned to Ashley's room only to find about six messages from Doug on the machine. We had obviously lost track of time. Ashley called Doug back, and I was to meet him and Gavin at the front desk of our dorm. I managed to pull myself together – I was almost always able to pull myself together in a pinch. I escorted Doug and Gavin up to our room where they eagerly gagged down the 'shrooms.

I remember us going here and there and everywhere that night – and everything being funny. Time and space don't really make normal sense when tripping. It's a vast shift in consciousness, to say the least. At some point we found ourselves hungry. Interestingly, I could eagerly eat on mushrooms but I never felt hungry on acid.

We ordered pizza to Gavin's dorm, and sat casually in the lobby, gobbling one slice after another as we people-watched – another favorite pastime while tripping. Hallucinating can be a mind-boggling experience – fantasy and reality merging amid bouts of seeing everything in slow motion, only to have everything speed up again like watching a VHS movie.

And then the DEA arrived. DEA as in Drug Enforcement Administration.

As the four of us were sitting there on a pair of dingy common-room couches in the lobby of Gavin's dorm, a group of fully dressed and armed DEA agents ran past us. Some ran to the left, going up the back flight of stairs. Some ran to the right, going up the other set of stairs. Several others stood waiting to take the elevator.

And we just sat and stared at them, along with the other students in the lobby. I was absolutely petrified – psychedelics will do that too, drastically amplifying whatever emotions might be present. Very slowly, I turned my head to look at my friends and their glassy red eyes with over-dilated pupils. We were silently freaking out.

Fully expecting the cops to reappear at any moment, accuse us of illegal drug use and throw us in some eternal prison hellhole, we sat there staring at each other. Finally, after what felt like an eternity, I slowly stood up and started to walk out of the building. My friends stood up and proceeded to exit the building with me. Pizza boxes abandoned on the lobby table.

I don't know how long it was before we spoke, or even took a breath, but that experience was terrifying enough to sober us all up pretty damn quick. Bummer. It had been a great trip up until then.

At some point the next day Ashley asked: "Did a bunch of DEA agents raid the dorm last night?"

"Yup." I said.

"Huh." Ashley responded.

Just another Friday night.

IN RETROSPECT

No, this behavior is/was not normal, but – and I'm just going to say it – it's fucking hilarious. It was ridiculous, reckless, and preposterous – and I mean those words in a good way.

NOTE: I'm not condoning this type of behavior, or suggesting anyone ingests a bag of mushrooms (with or without a peanut butter and jelly sandwich). I'm just able to look back at some of my experiences with a sense of humor and pleasure. That doesn't make me want to use drugs again ... it just makes me honest.

I still have the white and green cushioned lap tray. My family and I use it regularly to eat in front of the family room TV. I've cleaned off the resin stains, obviously, but the little marks and nicks from cutting and separating drugs are still there. And you can ever so faintly see

Ashley's name in black marker in the top left corner. I don't know how I ended up with it, or why I have kept it since December of 1995. I do know that when my kids are eating on the couch and I yell at them, "Don't make a mess - please get out the tray!" a little part deep inside of me chuckles at the sight of it.

|| The Red Zone ||

I was living the dream. I was attending this beautiful school, I had figured out my way around campus, secured my party friends, and procured my substance connections. And even better, since Cass had introduced me to her older brother Chris, I was able to be a regular part of the Sigma Phi Epsilon party scene.

They were great parties - like parties you'd see on a TV show and think, "That's not really how parties go. That's just Hollywood make-believe." But not these parties – every dorm-room door would be open with something exciting happening inside the room. Free alcohol was always provided, bong hits everywhere, people laughing, playing video games, or watching movies – and who knows what else was happening off in the dark corners. It was like a *Choose Your Own Adventure* book for a party. And there was always some strong alcohol punch at the end of the hallway in a gigantic trash can filled with whatever shit they put in it.

There was this one particular night when Sig Ep was having a big rager. I asked my drug buddies Ashley, Gavin, and Doug if they wanted to come, but they didn't really want to hang out with (what they considered to be) a bunch of drunk and rude frat boys. I didn't want to miss this party, so I decided to go alone. No big deal – I knew Chris and Matt and Josh, all frat guys I had partied with before.

I told Matt I would meet up with him before the party to eat some dinner in his frat room. I was pretty sure he liked me more than a friend. He was nice and cute and smart, and I'm not entirely sure why I didn't really go for him – maybe because he wasn't edgy enough or didn't like to get high. Anyway, I'd been smoking just prior to coming to this party, and I lost track of time and showed up about 45 minutes late. Matt was understandably annoyed.

"Jesus, Tracy, I expected you like an hour ago," he shouted at me as I entered his room.

"Sorry, I was getting ready and it took way longer than I thought."

He took one look at me and said, "You're crazy high again."

"Yessss," I smiled and batted my eyelashes, "aaaaaannnnd, I was getting ready for the party. See? Aren't I cute?" I forced a big smile while swaying my hips side to side.

"Whatever." He stood up and walked out of the room and left me alone.

Damnit, I thought to myself. Matt is nice, and this is no way to start the night. But there I was, showered, hair and makeup done – might as well carry on and make the most of the night. Besides, what else could I have done? Ashley, Gavin, and Doug were now off doing their own thing and I didn't know where they'd gone. This was a time before cell phones so I couldn't text them and say, "Where you at?"... so I decided to just jump in solo and choose my own adventure for the night – partying with some different people for a change.

As I walked down the hall, I saw that one room was set up like a bar, complete with some of the frat guys behind the tables mixing beverages for the guests. Lovely! This was better than the shitty beer I drank with Ashley. She liked beer, but not me. So I happily went up to the 'bartender' and ordered my favorite drink – Southern Comfort.

He said with his wide smile and Southern accent, "Yes, ma'am! And what would you like with your Southern Comfort?"

I looked him in the eye: "Ice, please."

After shooting my delicious cold drink in a few gulps I headed to the trash can at the end of the hall, grabbed myself a red solo cup, and scooped it in the sweet, sloppy mixture. I still felt bad about standing Matt up - these negative feelings weren't something I typically experienced. And I was excellent at staying as numb as possible to avoid them. In an effort to return to my safe happy numb place, I quickly downed my cup of jungle juice and went for another scoop before exploring the other rooms.

As I'm writing this, I'm floating high in the corner looking down at myself in that frat hallway, dipping my cup in the trash can for more. I want to cry out as an adult to my teen self, "Tracy, don't. Not another scoop into that bucket of booze, you stupid, stupid kid. It's disgusting and dangerous on so many levels. It's not normal or safe (or sanitary) in any way…. Please. Stop."

Eventually I landed in Josh's room. He was quiet and chill, sitting in there watching TV with a few other guys who were nonchalantly drinking and smoking a joint. I plopped down with the group and joined in.

Hit, hit, pass. Make idle chit chat. Laugh at the TV. This wasn't the rager I had expected, but it was getting the job done – I was feeling pretttttty good.

Time passed and one of the guys mentioned that the baggie was empty. My head started spiraling. I mean, we were out of drugs – why are they not taking this seriously? I was pretty hammered and high by now, and I became vocal about wanting more drugs. I leaned forward and started to pound on Josh's coffee table, chanting:

"More drugs, more drugs, more drugs!"

A kid across the table from me – I say kid because he looked really young, with messy dirty blonde hair and a baby face – said, "I've got a bit of pot back in my dorm."

This is where things went fuzzy. I don't remember the walk out of the frat and over to his dorm, but another guy from Josh's room came with us. I do have a flash vision of us sitting in a smaller dorm room, with me and the kid sitting on one of the twin beds and the other guy on the other bed. We were smoking a bowl, laughing occasionally, listening to some country music I wasn't familiar with (nor fond of).

And here's where my memory only comes back to me in short snippets, as if someone is turning a movie off and on. Pushing **PLAY** – then **STOP** – then **PLAY** again.

PLAY: I'm leaning back awkwardly against the wall, my neck bent in a weird direction, my legs hanging off the side of the bed. Now I'm being moved, kind of dragged to lie down flat on my back on the bed.

STOP.

PLAY: I can now feel someone close to me, leaning on me, their weight on top of me. I react, trying to wriggle my way out from under him but my legs are so heavy.

STOP.

PLAY: Someone is kissing me. Trying to kiss me. It feels like he's licking my face. I can smell his disgusting breath, a mixture of beer and smoke, right up against my nose.

STOP.

PLAY: I keep turning my head left and right to make him go away. I hear myself saying "Stop, stop, stop!" I'm pushing at his shoulders, pushing this disgusting guy away from me.

STOP.

PLAY: There are hands on me. I can feel that his shoulders are bare. He's sweaty and I'm trying to push him off of me, but my arms have no strength. I'm so weak! Why am I so weak? Why can't I work my arms? What's going on – why can't I open my eyes?

STOP.

***

The next thing I knew, a little bit of light was peeking around some curtains. I could tell it was early based on the grayness, not yellowness, of the light. But the little bit of light allowed me to see the room. I was still in that kid's dorm room and - I was in bed with him. His roommate was snoring across from us in the other twin bed. I was naked. I didn't move. My eyes frantically scanned the floor, looking for my clothes. Once I saw them, I started to construct a plan for how to get out of that room as quietly and as fast as possible. I strategized how I would remove myself from the bed and what item of clothing I would put on first and then next and then next.

I was able to leave the room without either of the boys waking up. I found my way to the elevator and went to the lobby to exit the building, then started to walk toward-my own dorm building. It was very chilly outside that early in the morning. I was walking in small swift steps. The heels of my boots clicked on the concrete walkway. My arms crossed tightly against my chest; I was squeezing myself. Squeezing myself because I was cold? Or because I was feeling seriously distraught?

I finally arrived back at my dorm and realized I didn't have my purse – I didn't even know where it was. I didn't remember seeing it on that kid's floor. I had to ask the person at the front desk to get my hall Residence Advisor (RA) to let me into my room. It was early, too early for me to have gone for a walk. And I certainly wouldn't have gone for a walk in that cute white top, light blue jeans, and brown boots.

This was clearly a walk of shame.

The girl at the front desk made a call and I met my hall RA by my room. She was not thrilled about the early request. I just said, "Sorry about this," and my eyes looked down at the floor as she let me into my dorm room. I could have had her let me into Ashley's room – the one I always stayed in – but I decided I wanted to be alone.

I thanked her, closed the door, took off my clothes, put on warm pajamas and climbed into my bed. I pulled the sheets and blanket tight around me, all the way up to my nose, covering my mouth.

My eyes were wide open – wider than I think they had ever been in my life. It was like I had seen something I shouldn't have seen. I was on high alert – not crying, not talking, not moving. Just absolutely frozen. I wasn't processing what had happened to me, or even the little nasty pieces I actually remembered. Instead, I was just ... blank.

I must have fallen asleep at some point because my dorm-room phone woke me up. I ignored it and tried to will myself back into unconsciousness. I didn't fall asleep, but I was also not awake. The phone rang again maybe an hour later. I still didn't answer it. Shortly after that, I heard a knock at my door.

"Tracy? Tracy, are you in there?"

It was Ashley. I gingerly made my way out of bed and let her into my room. "Hey," she said, "I've been trying to track you down! Looks like YOU had a long night!" She sounded so positive, excited to hear about the fun I was

supposed to have had. But then she really looked at me –
and could tell something was wrong. Her smile crashed.

"Oh no – what happened?" she asked in a quiet low voice.

I went back into my bed and pulled the sheets tight up
over me. She sat across from me on the other bed which
reminded me of the twin beds in the other dorm room –
me lying in bed with the kid whose name I never got, his
roommate sleeping across from us. Was he part of that too,
I wondered? I shuddered at that thought.

Ashley somehow knew to be quiet. She knew something
was very, very wrong. She just sat there across from me,
and eventually lay down on the bed without saying a
word, hands folded over her belly, ankles crossed.

And then after we lay there quietly for a good amount of
time, I started to tell her the bits and pieces that I
remembered. I was somehow talking clearly without any
emotion at all, simply relaying the facts. I paused and
looked over at her at some point. She was still lying on her
back, staring up at the ceiling. I saw tears running down
the side of her face into her blonde hair. She hadn't said a
word. She was just there with me as I relayed this horrific,
horrific event.

Seeing her tears made me start to cry. She got up and
came over to my bed. I scooted over, closer to the wall.
She climbed under the covers and faced me - her forehead
resting against my forehead, and her left hand gently
caressing my arm in an attempt to soothe me.

She finally said, barely a whisper: "What can I do?"

I didn't know which of us felt more helpless in that moment. "Nothing," I said. "There is nothing to do."

I knew that I wasn't going to report the rape or even tell anyone except Ashley. I could play out in my head the probable conversation with the campus police:

"You were where? You were doing what? You had how much to drink? How old are you? So you got high at the fraternity and then left with someone you don't know? You went back to their dorm to get more pot? What did the shirt look like that you were wearing? How tight were your jeans?"

These would have been the questions I'd be asked. Would they have seen me as the victim? Would they have taken pity on me or just judged me, considering my forbidden state of intoxication? Would anything actually have been done? I didn't even know that kid's fucking name. No, I didn't have a case against him. Well, I didn't *feel* like I had a case.

As so often happens with rape, during the next couple of days, instead of using the little energy I had to focus on what a complete piece of shit this (name unknown) kid was, I started to question myself.

- Why did I drink that much? I never drink that much! Stupid! How many scoops of that drink did I have? What was in that drink? Was I drugged or did I just allow myself to get too wasted?
- Why did I go with him? I didn't even know him! Did I really need to get MORE high?!

- What did I think would happen going to a frat party by myself, dressed in that cute little white top? None of my friends were there. I barely know those frat-guys!
- Why couldn't I push him away? Why couldn't I fight back? I should have tried harder. I should have pushed harder. I should have shouted STOP louder!
- Was it just him, that kid whose bed I woke up in? Or was it his roommate too? He was there in the room. Did he ... also?

For three days, the scenes of that night and these aching questions constantly ran through my head, over and over like torture.

After the first day I moved myself back into Ashley's room where I usually slept in the other bed – but I didn't get out of bed to go anywhere that Saturday or Sunday. Ashley kindly would only speak to me when spoken to. She brought me food from the cafeteria, most of which would go uneaten. We got high together that Sunday afternoon – and I was surprised by how little I cared or even wanted to do it.

On Monday I didn't go to my classes. Later that afternoon, after Ashley got back from her classes, she suggested a shower. I felt like I had enough energy and strength to get through a shower, so I quietly and slowly joined her walking down the hallway to the bathrooms, shower-tote hanging loosely in my hand. I took a long hot shower, washing, and rewashing, and rewashing myself like a snake trying to shed a layer of skin and hopefully coming out new on the other side.

The shower helped. On Monday evening I ate with Ashley in the room. We got high and she did something - I don't remember what – that actually made me laugh. But the laughter felt foreign, almost like I was cheating on my despair. But it also felt good, like a mini breakthrough, a window opening up to normalcy – whatever normalcy meant.

I attended classes on Tuesday but I felt like a cloud was hanging over my head, following me as I walked around campus. I felt like I must be looking different, dirty, like people knew what had happened to me. And I also found my eyes darting anxiously left and right, looking for that kid, hoping, praying I wouldn't run into him. Would I even recognize him?

As I continued to put one foot in front of the other, I got through the next day, and the next. I started to feel a bit better. I tried to act normal. I asked Ashley to please not tell Gavin or Doug. I didn't want them to know and look at me differently.

I avoided having sex with Gavin for a long time. He never once questioned me or forced the subject with me. Good for him. We were young and stupid, but he was a gentleman about such things. And I was thankful I was on the pill so there would be no pregnancy issues. I (irresponsibly) didn't get tested for STDs until years later. Luckily, I was in the clear.

I found my purse about two weeks later, just before leaving for Thanksgiving break. After a Psych 101 class Josh said, "Hey, I think you left your purse on my floor at a party a while back."

I asked if I could walk with him back to the fraternity and get it. I wanted someone with me. And as I walked down the hallway of the fraternity, I noticed how dirty and smelly the place actually was. It was like a veil had been removed and I could see it all clearly for the first time – it was just a shitty frat house. No magic here.

I grabbed my purse off Josh's floor in a corner where it must have remained unmoved for the last two weeks. I then continued down the hallway to see if Matt was there. His door was open, and he was on his couch, reading. I knocked on the door frame, and he looked up and smiled.

"Hi!" he said, looking hopeful.

I was quiet for a bit, breathing, still standing there in his doorway. His smile faded.

"I'm sorry... I'm just – I'm sorry." I nodded at him, gave him a half smile, and walked away. I would later see Matt in passing here and there on campus before winter break, but we didn't talk again.

Leaving to go home for Thanksgiving break was a relief. I had barely been getting myself up and together for the previous two weeks, and it would be good to get away from campus. It would be nice to see my high school friends and hear how they were doing. It would be nice to eat my grandmother's delicious food. It might even be nice to have my grandfather ask me a million questions and give me his advice on my life – at least he cared. And yeah, it might be nice to see my mom's beautiful blue eyes and get a warm hug from her.

But the thing I looked forward to the most was cuddling with my dog Ruffles. Her fluffy white fur, warmth, and unconditional love were what I needed most right then. I would fill up on all of this, then return to campus to finish out the semester before winter break.

"I've got this," I told myself.

IN RETROSPECT

It hadn't been my fault. None of it was my fault – the drinking or drugging or wearing a cute white top. NOT. MY. FAULT. Not even one tiny part of this situation was my fault. I was dumb and naïve, a fawn on wobbly legs walking around that giant campus. I will accept responsibility for my many lousy and dangerous decisions ... but not this.

The term "Red Zone" refers to a specific period during the first few months of freshman year in college when a higher number of sexual assaults and other forms of sexual misconduct tend to occur. In fact, more than 50% of college sexual assaults occur between August to

November of a students' freshman year. Little did I know I was just another freshman assault in the "Red Zone."

Of course, I'm just one story. There are millions of women who could tell their own story. Sexual assault is real and much more common than people think – and it's happening to people we know and love.

I'm deeply grateful that I've had a healthy and vibrant sex life for many years. Both before my husband with loving boyfriends, and especially with my husband of almost twenty years. I've enjoyed great sex – the rape did not and does not define me. I thankfully barely think about it today. But still – it happened and it's a real and painful part of my history.

|| The Library, the Cops, and a Turtle ||

Unlike in high school, I was not a quality student at the University of South Carolina ... and that's putting it lightly. There were multiple classes I attended occasionally, and some classes I did not attend at all. I didn't drop them from my schedule, I just stopped going. But I did enjoy my Exercise Science major, and, oddly enough, cared about my performance in those particular classes.

I found myself pulling back just a bit from the raucous party scene when I returned from Thanksgiving Break. The assault had obviously, understandably, soured my 'all-in' attitude. Don't get me wrong, I was still using – but I was more cautious about who I was around.

It was almost the end of the semester before Christmas break, and I had a huge paper due in one of my Exercise Science classes. I had been in the library all day long doing research and typing up the paper. This was unusual for me – I rarely did any work at USC, let alone spend hour upon hour in the library.

I had maybe one more hour of work to complete, but I was starving. I left my books and papers and book-bag in the little cubby at the library and walked over to the student cafeteria for a late dinner. I was fried – 'exhausted' fried, not 'high' fried. While I was in the line getting food, Izzy, a girl from my dorm, came over to me and asked, "What happened to Ashley? We saw the cops. Do you know what happened?"

My stomach dropped and I could instantly feel my heart beating in my throat. I tried to swallow. "What cops? What do you mean? When did this happen?"

"I don't know", Izzy said, "maybe 30 minutes ago? They were still there when we left the dorm to get food."

I left my tray in line and ran out of the cafeteria. My mind was racing – what did she do? Who was with her? Where was she now? What was in the room? Where were our drugs hidden? Shit. Shit. Shit.

I saw a campus police car parked at the far side of the dorm. I walked in, trying to catch my breath and seem as casual as possible, flashed my ID to the front desk and walked on to the elevator.

Breathe, focus – breathe, focus. I tried hard to calm and reassure myself on the long ride up. These were the slowest elevators ever! My room was on the top floor, the 8th floor. DING! The elevator doors opened and I saw Cass (remember her?) standing in her doorway directly across from the elevator. As soon as she saw me her eyes widened. She looked me directly in the eye and slowly shook her head – NO. And with zero words exchanged, I knew I should not get off that elevator.

That was when I heard a loud deep voice say, "Hello? Excuse me. Hello?"

I pushed the lobby button and door-close button as quickly as possible. As the doors were just shutting, I saw the cop coming around the corner into view. The door closed – but these goddamn elevators were so slow, I knew the cop would easily make it to the lobby before me.

Hell, he could probably go get a donut and return before I got there!

I looked at what floor I was on, and immediately pushed the next floor button. The elevator stopped at the 4th floor. I hopped off, darted to the right, and ran to the set of stairs at the back of the building. I ran down those stairs – more like fell down those stairs – and burst out the side door.

The cop was already outside, walking fast around the corner. He saw me bolt through the side door.

"Hey! Kid! Stop!" His voice was closer than I liked.

No fucking way was I stopping. Like Forrest Gump, I ... Was ... Running! But so was the cop. I knew not to waste time or energy looking back. I could hear him breathing heavily. I could feel the sweatshirt I had borrowed from Amy swish and sway on my back, the hood bouncing like crazy. And then I felt a hand grabbing at my ponytail, then grabbing the bouncing hood of Amy's sweatshirt.

As he yanked on the hood to stop me, I spontaneously relaxed my arms backward and simply let it pull right off of my back. This caused the cop to stumble, not expecting to grasp at air – and I was able to keep going. I continued running, headed for the only place off-campus that I could think of – Amy and Charlie's apartment half a mile away.

When I got there, I told them what little I knew, not having any idea what had actually happened or what possible trouble Ashley was in. Charlie drove me back to campus to get my bag from the library before it closed, and I spent the night at their place.

***

The next day, after I went to my Exercise Science class and turned in my final paper, I ventured back to the dorm, assuming the coast was clear by now. When I got to our room, to Ashley's room, she wasn't there. I went to the floor RA, Mary, and asked her if she knew what had happened. Mary was cool – I knew I didn't have to play games with her. Here's what she relayed to me:

Ashley had had a party in our room, which wasn't out of the ordinary. However, I gather she had gotten too drunk to walk our friend Gavin back down to the front desk as was required with male visitors – check in, check out. On this night, Ashley couldn't even stand or be coherent enough to escort Gavin down to the lobby, so he went down by himself. When he was questioned by the front desk, he said Ashley was sick and couldn't come down.

That obviously raised some questions, and one of the head RAs was sent to go check on her. Upon entering her room, I'm certain they had quite a shock to their senses. The beer cans, all of the art/graffiti we had drawn on the walls, the stench of pot, the cigarettes that littered the tiny patio, the bongs and bowls and rolling papers scattered among the room – for Ashley and me, it was a non-stop party. But the party stopped here.

Campus police were called, and some girls on our floor were interviewed. My name came up as a likely host, or certainly guest, of this particular party. However, since I wasn't seen that night and wasn't caught in or outside the building (phew!), they couldn't really stick anything on me. And *technically* it wasn't actually my dorm room according to the official records.

Ashley had obviously messed up. She got too wasted and couldn't follow the rules – she couldn't cover her tracks. She loved to drink A LOT, and drinking made her sloppy. That's where I usually came in – I was the one to tell her when to stop or to take care of her. I was completely fucked up all the time but almost never sloppy. I hated feeling out of control ... and I always had a plan.

I was pissed at Ashley but also scared for her. When she came back to the dorm room late the next afternoon, after having spent the night in jail, she and I hugged and cried. She was going to be fined quite a lot of money, and worse still, kicked out of school. Meanwhile, I would be totally okay – no charges, no trouble. Why? Because when Ashley was questioned by the cops, questioned about all of the drugs and paraphernalia in the room, she could have shared the weight of that punishment with me – but she didn't. Ashley claimed everything was hers. Everything.

As we sat there cross-legged facing each other, our foreheads leaning against one another, I told her how much I loved her – and how I owed her, like, BIG TIME. And through tears she said, "I love you so much." And we did. We were two stupid, druggy, drunk, irresponsible girls, but I loved her so deeply – loved her humor, her sarcasm, her wit and energy. I loved how she played guitar, and how artistic she was. I loved her loud raspy laugh. I hated her large sloppy tie-dye T-shirts. I hated that she smoked cigarettes. And I hated her boyfriend, Doug. But that was it. All the rest was love.

Ashley loved turtles. She always wore this one gold turtle necklace. On the last day of school before her parents arrived to collect her, she took it off and gave it to me.

"I will never, ever, forget you," she said as she placed her turtle necklace inside my hand and closed my fingers around it.

Our party was over.

A NOTE TO ASHLEY

I've tried hard to find you over the years, but I can't. I don't know where you are, who you are, or what's become of you. But I think of you often and I miss you. I want to see you and hug you and say thank you. For that short amount of time we had together, thank you for being a beautiful friend and special person. Thank you for putting me back together more than once and protecting me against legal complications.

I still have your necklace. It hangs with my other jewelry, and whenever I look at it I remember you. I have a picture of us together in my bedside table. I will never forget you. I say your name every day. Multiple times a day.

My firstborn daughter is named Ashley.

|| Minnesota, eh? ||

After my assault and after I found out a couple of my close campus friends wouldn't be returning to USC due to poor behavior or grades – and knowing that my own school performance would prove to be less than stellar – I decided not to return to USC. My mom, who was worried about my depressed mood, fully supported this decision.

This was actually a terrifying time. I was leaving the freedom of college, where I could do drugs and drink whenever and wherever. I was leaving a friend that I really loved and connected with. I didn't just feel like a failure, I knew I was a failure. I knew my grades were terrible (I left that first semester with a 1.4 GPA), and I knew I was not making responsible decisions on my own.

But I also didn't know how I was going to live in my house again, with my mom, Mum-Mum, and Pop-Pop. How would I be able to get stoned? How would I hide my drugs? Would I be transferring to another school? Could I even transfer to another school? Would I have to get a job? What would my high school friends think? I could come up with no new plan for my life. There was no good answer – I was out of moves …

And then the decision was made for me.

The day after Christmas (because we can't ruin Christmas) my mom knocked on the door of my bedroom to speak with me.

"It's obvious this, well, this thing with you has gotten worse," she started, unable to actually say the word addiction or drugs. It was just 'a thing' of mine.

"Okay. What thing?" I reply, with a look of confusion.

"This, this ... your using drugs." There – she'd finally said it. "I'm sure you're using them. Your friend got in trouble at school for having drugs. I know you two were close, so you were probably in on it." Speaking to me like this was hard for her – she generally avoided confrontation and arguments at all costs. 'Keep the peace' was how she'd been brought up.

"Well, yeah, sometimes, sure," I countered. "But mostly I just had fun watching them. I mean, yeah, of course I have done stuff, like everybody else. But I'm nothing like them."

She looked at me and said right back – "Tracy, I don't believe you."

Time to turn it up. "Don't believe me – what do you mean?" I stood up from my bed, walking closer to her. "It's not like you have any proof, or whatever, that I'm doing all this stuff you seem to think I'm doing."

"Tracy. You can't be serious. I know you were doing some of this stuff in high school. Your friends were worried about you and once shared some concerns with me. And I can certainly see, based on the last few months, that you are definitely using some type of drug. Look at your friends, your grades, the trouble you've been around. And you definitely didn't seem yourself at Thanksgiving – we barely saw you." She actually said this quite calmly, seeming resolute in her beliefs.

Fuck.

"I agree, it was a bad semester. I sucked. Okay? I didn't do so well being on my own, but now I know how to do it. Now that I didn't do well, I know what I have to do to be better. I'll just move forward at a different school. It'll be fine." I could feel my brain spinning, pushing out these words.

She took a deep breath. "I've made a decision. I've talked to some people, and I think – we think – that going to rehab at this point would be the best step for you." She said each word slowly, like it had been practiced.

My blood pressure went through the roof. "Rehab!? Mom... You've got to be kidding me!" I started laughing.

She continued speaking evenly. "I've done some research and found a place that works well with teenagers. You will be leaving on Friday."

"Leaving on Friday to go where? What do you even mean? You can't be serious about this!" I stopped laughing.

"It's called Hazelden. It's in Minnesota."

"What the fuck – Minnesota!?"

"Tracy. Calm down. I've made the decision. I've purchased your ticket, and they have a spot for you. You will be leaving Friday morning and flying to Minnesota. You'll stay in an inpatient program for thirty days."

I blacked out. I stopped pacing and stood by my large bedroom window, just staring blankly out. My head was bombarded with questions and fears. We stood there in silence for some time. I'd finally been caught – and worse still, my mom was going to do something about it. What could I do? What could I possibly say to convince her otherwise? And what other option did I have!? Could I just leave the house, like, run away? And go where?

No - I was out of moves.

She grabbed the large suitcase that had been sitting in the hallway and put it on my bed. "You still have a couple of days to decide what to pack. It's cold out there right now, so please pack warm clothing. Let me know if there's anything you don't have that you may need. We can talk more about this later."

Then she left my room and closed my door.

I continued to stand at the window, looking out like I was staring from inside a jail cell. Life as I had known it would be changed – but then I had to admit, life as I currently knew it wasn't going exactly as I had planned either. And right then, while my head was frantically searching for something to hold on to, some plan to get out of this predicament – I had an epiphany.

First of all, I suddenly accepted and even embraced the fact that I was not going to get out of this. Nope. My mom was legitimately holding the cards. I *would* be getting on that plane on Friday to Minnesota where I would spend thirty days at a fucking rehab. And accepting that this would be the month of January, 1996, I decided to look at it as a time to cleanse myself. Yeah, a cleansing – like a retreat. Spa rehab! New year, new me!

I turned to my mirror. Seeing myself honestly, I did look pretty banged up. My skin was yellowish, I had a deep blackish color under my eyes, my nails and hair were brittle and dried out, my index finger and thumb always had burns on them, and the thick resin pot-smoke coating inside my lungs had made running harder and harder. Maybe, just maybe, a little time away would actually do me some good. And here came the bonus – I figured that, after thirty days away from drugs, when I came back, the high would be absolutely amazing.

But I still had over 48 hours before I had to get on that plane, and I was going to make the most of it. Besides, I would have to celebrate my own New Year's Eve early with my friends before I left. I felt pretty certain the rehab center wouldn't exactly be rolling out the keg on December 31st.

By the time my mom took me to the airport on Friday morning I was in rough shape after the last couple of nights. Mom hadn't said much of anything to me during those last two days – she hadn't tried to fight against me going out with my friends and I hadn't tried to hide it.

We were sitting there waiting for the plane to board. This was a time when non-ticketed family members could wait with you at the gate. I could see that her eyes were wet, and she was now lovingly rubbing my back with her hand. I was ignoring her, listening to my cassette player, too tired and too angry at her to argue... or accept her love. What's done was done. My flight started boarding, and I gave her a quick goodbye kiss on the cheek.

The flight was uneventful; I slept most of the way. When we landed, I made my way to baggage claim – a cavernous, industrial-lit space surprisingly empty considering I was traveling during the Christmas holidays. I suddenly felt small and very alone, a stranger in a strange place. But then I was met by someone who worked at Hazelden, there to pick up myself and two other kids – a guy and another girl. The guy seemed a little bit older than me, and the girl a little bit younger. We greeted each other but didn't say much.

Outside it was cold – painfully cold! The ride to Hazelden wasn't too long and, before I knew it, I was wheeling my luggage into the rehab lobby to get checked in. This wasn't like the check-in at some hotel – it involved a full body-cavity search. Okay, maybe I'm being a little extreme, no fingers were stuffed up my asshole. But my bag was thoroughly searched. And if you're wondering, no, I didn't bring any drugs with me. I'm not that stupid.

A counselor took me to my room, which I was to share with five other girls. UGH. I was assigned to a twin bed and one small standing closet with two drawers. On a sterile end table was a reading lamp plus some pamphlets and the 'Big Book,' which I'd soon find out was the Bible of AA – Alcoholics Anonymous.

I was given a short amount of time to unpack and get somewhat settled. Then the counselor returned to go over the rehab's expectations and daily routine. As she read me the schedule, which started with 7:30 a.m. wakeup call, I started to think this might be harder than I had thought. And then I was told about the daily chores we would all be expected to complete – what? UGH! This wasn't quite the pampering I had hoped for.

After hearing what was expected of me on a daily basis at this absurd nightmare boot-camp rehab-spa, I was taken to another counselor for an initial one-on-one assessment. Dennis was going to be my main counselor for my group and individual sessions. He was in his 50s, a bit heavy with glasses. For some reason I noticed he was wearing a lot of browns with corduroy pants. Gross.

He asked me a bunch of questions about when I started using, what I used, how often, how I used it – shit like that. I told him maybe 50% truths. I obviously didn't arrive here on good behavior so I figured I might as well fess up a little bit. As he was writing something on his notepad, I noticed he was left-handed.

"I'm left-handed too," I shared. Lefties tend to notice each other – we're only 11% of the world population.

"That doesn't surprise me," he responded. "A huge percentage of addicts are left-handed." Okay, Dennis, I thought. What the fuck do you want me to do with that? Whatever.

It was finally time for lunch, and I met up with the other (well, what – patients?) in the cafeteria. I grabbed some cereal and sat down at a table with a few other people. They looked pretty much like kids I would hang out with, somewhere between preppy and hippy, not crazy goth or with purple hair – just kids in jeans and t-shirts. We ran through introductions and I found out that two of them, the guys, had already been there for a few weeks. The girl had just finished her first week. I listened to them and looked around the room at my fellow 'inmates.' So this was what drug addicts look like? I'm not sure what I was expecting, but everybody kind of looked like some version of me.

After more meetings and groups and tours and reading pamphlets, it was finally time for bed. I was feeling exhausted and fell asleep. The sound of an alarm clock going off at 7:30 a.m. was jarring. And the routine was exhausting – completing some menial tasks, then breakfast, morning group session, private reading time, snack, topic group talk, lunch, one-on-one chat, more group sessions – yuck!

The next few days were similar – group meetings, therapy, readings, food, chores. I was miserable. And then on Day Four I was hit with an added pressure. Maybe I was just particularly sensitive on this New Year's Day, 1996 – pissed off by the fact that'd just spent New Year's Eve in fucking rehab. Maybe some of my chipper rehab peers were annoying me. Maybe I was fed up by being awoken at 7:30 in the morning yet again. Maybe the shit my counselor was saying was getting to me. Maybe the freezing weather in Nowhere, Minnesota was depressing.

All I knew was that I felt like I was going to burst – like something was growing on the inside of me and trying to push out, like the alien popping out of that guy's stomach in that movie … conveniently named *Alien* (1979). I felt like I was going to implode and explode at the same time. Everything, and I mean everything, was rubbing me the wrong way.

Psssst, Tracy – that's called withdrawal.

In the three years I had been doing drugs, I had never gone more than 36 hours without being on something – anything – so this was new for me. If I was coming off of one substance, I would mask those symptoms by taking another substance ... so this felt fucking terrible.

The Hazeldon doctors also let me know that my bloodwork showed extremely high levels of THC ... so much for trying to hide my usage with half-truths. They told me that the significant amount of weed I had been consuming over the past several years (in addition to all the other drugs I was abusing regularly) had actually created a physical addiction. Something about my brain adapting to all of the pot in my system by changing the chemicals it produced. Blah, blah, blah ... all I remember hearing was that the next few weeks could turn out to be quite unpleasant.

To distract myself and have a little bit of fun, I decided to talk my group-therapy 'inmates' into coming up with funny ways to mess with Dennis. When we entered the group room, everybody sat in a different seat than usual, we all sat weirdly or awkwardly, and we didn't say a word. And every time Dennis asked a question we responded with "I don't know."

But this didn't go over well. Dennis didn't find our little game entertaining. No sense of humor at all around here!

The next day, I felt worse – worse physically and worse emotionally. I hadn't felt much of anything emotionally in years at this point because feelings, well, they suck. I refused to do my morning chores, and I became more disruptive in group. Then the next day I lost it. I felt so physically uncomfortable, and I didn't know what to do with my body. I couldn't sit still - it felt like I was being pulled in a million directions, my mind unable to hold a train of thought.

And then I started to recall things that had been stuffed way down inside of me for a long time – buried in the festering trash can of my life. But now it began creeping into my mind – I was smelling the vomity stink of those buried memories. Fuck. With no substances to press it down, the lid was coming off.

And then something happened. I don't remember the exact question that Dennis asked that day in afternoon group – but it was just too much for me to process. So I got up, grabbed my crappy, uncomfortable metal chair, and hurled it at him. I remember him dodging the chair, the chair banging into the side of his desk, and things being knocked over on the desk and falling to the floor. I remember the silence in the room – and Dennis's wide eyes looking at me from behind his thick, dorky glasses.

After a moment of silence and probably shock, he quickly walked out of the room and returned moments later with two other Hazelden workers. "Tracy. You'll be coming with me immediately."

Ooooo, scary Dennis came out to play.

I exited the room, kicking a trash can and shit over as I went, taking my one last stand. Stand against what? I didn't know. I just knew I needed to punch something to get this fuming, wound-up feeling out of me.

The two workers - maybe the better word is 'orderlies' - brought me past the front desk and down a short hall. They opened up the white metal door to a room on the left and told me to go in and wait there. And as I walked into this weird room, looking around at the thick gray walls and cot in the far corner, I heard the door close solidly behind me.

It took me a few moments to put it all together, but I suddenly realized that I was locked in a padded cell. Like, literally. I walked over to a wall and pushed on it. Hard foam, but foam.

So there I was, locked in this padded room. Alone. Caged like an insane criminal in solitary confinement with absolutely nothing to do, no distractions, just me and my thoughts. And yeah, I suddenly had thoughts, loads of them. I was a swirling ball of feelings – furious, scared, confused ... and sad. Ridiculously, desperately, and frighteningly sad.

At some point I found myself hugging my thighs, back against the padded wall, rocking back and forth to dispel these feelings – trying to somehow ignore my years of buried trash. Then, without warning, after my brain had run through its usual twists and turns of excuses and avoidance, its plans and lies to figure out my next move, I heard a question that I wasn't expecting.

"Where did I go wrong?"

I started to think back over the progression of my drug use. "What had gone wrong, when had things gone bad – had it been the crack? Maybe that was my problem. Or maybe it had been the acid? The mushrooms? I'd heard they can mess up your brain. Maybe it was that. Maybe the acid but not the mushrooms? Alcohol? Maybe booze but not beer? Had I tried just too many things? Was it the pills I'd tried? Ecstasy? Or the occasional bumps of coke?"

As I ran through my rather long list of drugs, trying to pinpoint the "problem drug," I began to see my crooked path a little more clearly. And then the whispering voice inside me said: "Tracy. It's not one thing. It's all the things. *It's everything.*"

I didn't know who or what had said that – but they were wrong. They had to be wrong. I wasn't ready or willing to stop taking them all – no. No. No. Shut up.

And the next day I made the reckless decision to get myself out of Hazleton. I was 19 years old, so legally I could sign myself out. I got on the phone with my mom.

"Mom! They are crazy here – for no reason they locked me up in a fucking padded cell last night. This is ridiculous – I'm not doing this."

"Your counselor phoned and told me what happened," she responded. "He and the staff were very upset; they're really worried about you and want you to stay." Her voice cracked at the end, like she was crying.

"No way I'm staying, Mom. You said I had a return ticket – I'm coming home."

There was a pause. "I can't stop you from signing yourself out. But if that is your decision, you are not allowed back in the house. Dennis said you have a real problem. You are one of the worst kids he has seen. He said if I let you back in the house, I'd be enabling your problem."

"Well, then, fuck you! And fuck Dennis! I can get by on my own, I'll be fine, I have friends… You won't hear from me!"

I slammed down the phone.

I looked at the lady behind the front desk. With a cocky sense of entitlement, I said to her: "I believe my mother has a return flight ticket for me? Can someone take me to the airport? I'm leaving. Now." I stomped back to my room and threw all of my belongings into my suitcase. I remember some of my roommates trying to talk to me. I remember Dennis trying to talk to me. I don't know what he said. I stayed silent, packed my shit as fast as I could, and got out of there.

As promised, I was given a ticket and a ride to the airport. I landed in Philadelphia with no plan, no home. Just my suitcase and me, standing there in the dingy, smelly – but familiar – PHL airport, looking at the payphone. Finally, I dialed someone I hadn't talked to in months. Someone who was not good for me to be around but someone who I was sure still loved me, someone who would help me – and he would definitely have drugs.

"Hey, Mitch. It's me, Tracy."

IN RETROSPECT

With marijuana/THC (vapes, gummies, drops, joints, etc.) becoming more widely used and accepted in our society today, people sometimes question whether I was actually addicted to marijuana. For decades I heard, "But pot isn't addictive."

In previous years it was believed that cannabis was not a habit-forming substance. However, scientists have now determined that with consistent heavy use, the human brain can become dependent on pot for key functions ... and stopping it can result in significant withdrawal effects.

I found this out the hard way 30 years ago, and it was glaringly apparent to my counselors and rehab centers at the time. I'm glad to see that the science and evidence have been publicized by the NIH and CDC, and the official diagnosis of 'Cannabis Use Disorder' is now represented in the DSM-5.

|| The Cold & The Heat ||

I sat in PHL baggage claim for a couple of hours before Mitch was able to come pick me up. I'd spent the two hours trying to figure out where to go, where to stay – but I'd come up empty. It's not like I could knock on Beth's door and say "Hey, any chance I could crash here for a bit? Oh – why am I not staying at home? Because I'm a junkie who just signed myself out of rehab and I have nowhere to go. Cool if I stay with you?" No – I was pretty sure that wouldn't fly.

The interaction with Mitch in the car on the way back to the suburbs was strained. The last time we talked was shortly after I had jumped out of his car after getting in a fight, followed by having to go to the hospital for an infection in my foot. We didn't exactly end on good terms – but then again, desperate times call for desperate measures.

Eventually Mitch asked the question I had been hoping he would ask: "Do you wanna smoke a bowl?"

"Yeah, thanks. That would be great actually." I tried to stay neutral, but after over a week without any drugs, every nerve ending stood up when I heard the word "bowl."

He already had a bowl packed which he pulled out of the glove compartment. He started driving with his knee as he lit it and took a big hit. Mitch then passed me the bowl. I flicked on the lighter and started to suck – and a sense of pure relief washed over me, like that feeling just before falling asleep. The stress of the day is over, everything is done, and that sweet reprieve of sleep arrives.

I spent the ride home telling Mitch about the last couple of months. I didn't go into detail about South Carolina and my experiences and friends there. I pretty much just shared how things didn't work out and I decided not to return to school – and then how my mom decided to send me to rehab, and how I signed myself out, and now here I was ... with nowhere to go.

After having that apartment for a year, Mitch wasn't making ends meet and had to move back home with his parents. So that was that – staying with Mitch was pretty much out.

"Oh," I say. "Well, maybe I can just tag along to whatever party you are going to tonight and I can figure something out later."

And like old times, we continued on to Luke's house for the party. That whole night is a bit of a blur. It's amazing how even a week away from drugs made everything stronger, more intense. It honestly would have felt wonderful if I didn't have this looming homelessness hanging over me. I ended up spending the night in Luke's basement. Luke woke me up early, before his parents would be coming home. It was too early to call Mitch. I had appreciated him picking me up from the airport and didn't want to totally burn that bridge, so I decided to walk to a local food store. It wasn't far from Luke's, maybe one and a half miles. What was weird, however, was that

I was dragging my suitcase behind me. That was all I had – my suitcase leftover from rehab. Luckily, I'd packed very warm clothes for Minnesota and was prepared for the cold January of suburban Philadelphia.

I bought myself a plain bagel from the bakery and ate it on a bench inside the store. Along with the plane ticket home, my mom had left me $30. I was going to have to be very careful to make this $30 last. Around 10:00 a.m., I called Mitch, who picked me up about an hour later. Steve and Adam were in the car, and we drove around Valley Forge Park and got high as if no time had passed, like everything was normal...

But it wasn't. With each drink or hit or bump or whatever, I couldn't shake that little voice in my head, the same one that spoke to me in the padded room telling me that it was "all the things" I was doing that were the problem. But I was still managing to push that voice away, telling myself, "Hey, I can figure this out. I always have and I aways will." I was not ready to believe that voice yet.

For the next few weeks I did anything but "figure it out." My suitcase and I bounced around here and there. I would walk along the safer and quieter streets and find a 'nice' shed to sleep in. But it was cold, so sometimes Mitch or one of his friends would sneak me into their basements for the night. And yeah, more than once I had to do 'favors' for these 'friends' – favors as a thank you for sharing some drugs or food or a warm basement to sleep in. Favors you never, ever want to imagine your daughter doing.

On one particular night I found myself walking around the local strip mall in a generally safe part of town. It was late ... and cold. I'd tried to open about five cars, waiting for an alarm to go off or someone to see me and ask what I was doing. I finally found a beat-up Toyota sedan that was unlocked behind the ACME, a local grocery chain. I climbed into the back and threw some of my extra clothes on top of me to get warmer. Fuck it was cold! As I was balled up, shivering, I hoped the owner of this car wasn't coming back soon, and if they did that they wouldn't freak out.

And it was in the back of that miserable Toyota that my homelessness hit me the hardest. First, memories of happier times early in my childhood started to rush over me, and I began to ache with what I can only describe as being homesick. Homesick for the ease, love, and softness from my life – a life before Richard.

That of course led me to thoughts of the home I was currently locked out of. The light-yellow-colored walls of my bedroom, the warmth and comfort of my bed. I thought about my mom and the conversation we had when I yelled at her from rehab. I couldn't believe she refused to let me come home. How was she? Was she worried about me? She must have been freaking out by then.

To defend myself from these guilty feelings and present predicament, I started thinking, "Fuck her! I don't really want to be with her anyway. She did this to me!" The only reason I would have wanted to go home was to spend time with Ruffles. She was the only one that hadn't been an asshole. I wanted to feel her softness and heat. And then I thought about my grandparents, Mum-Mum and Pop-Pop. I wondered what they knew, and what they must have been thinking. I wondered what my mom had told them.

I'd called my mom twice since I had gotten back to Philly. I did this for selfish reasons, of course. I wanted to make her feel remorseful when she heard my voice. I also wanted to let her know who to contact to track me down if (and when) she wanted me to come home. But on these calls my mom didn't say much – our conversations were short. She might swallow a cry. I'd take a deep breath. But neither of us gave in.

I decided before I fell asleep in that cold beat-up Toyota behind the ACME that maybe I needed to take it up a notch. Maybe I needed to visit the house.

The next evening, I had Mitch drive me to my house. I didn't want her to see me with him, so I asked him to wait in the car around the corner. I didn't expect to be long.

I went up and knocked on the door, and I heard Ruffles bark in the background. This made me smile.

My mom's face looked out of the window on the left side of the door to see who it was. She slowly and hesitantly opened the door and looked at me standing there.

"Hi," I said.

"Hi," she replied. She was blocking the doorway. She hadn't invited me in.

"I was wondering if I could grab a few things from my room."

"Yes. I suppose that's fine. I will come with you." She was almost robotic. It felt like we were playing a game of talking chicken, like, the person who said too much first would lose.

"Okay," I said.

As I put my foot up on the step to walk in and my mom slowly moved to the side, I saw Ruffles sitting at the bottom of the stairs, her tail wagging, banging against the floor. But she didn't move. I could tell she was happy to see me but she was also on high alert, unsure of whose side to take or what to do. She sat patiently and calmly by the stairs until I came over to pet her. I rubbed her face and massaged her ears as she licked me. I started to feel pressure well up in my chest and my eyes water. I had to pull back. I couldn't fall apart. I had to appear together.

I heard my grandmother call out from her TV room, "Tracy! Tracy, is that you?"

I suddenly felt unprepared to deal with my grandparents. "Umm, Hi, Mum-Mum, yeah, it's me. I just came to grab some stuff. I'll be with you in a minute."

I continued to walk upstairs, my mom following me silently. As I turned the corner at the top of the stairs, I saw that my bedroom door was closed with a note taped to the door. In black sharpie marker my mom had written

"DO NOT TOUCH ANYTHING." I turned around, made silent eye contact with her, and then continued toward my bedroom. My door was unlocked and I went in.

To be honest, I hadn't stopped at the house to get stuff from my bedroom, but I decided I might as well grab some clean clothes. I made myself look busy and threw some clean clothes on my bed. My mom was watching my every move. I waved my arms over the clothes and said, "Okay, mother?" I was such an asshole.

She cleared her throat. "Yes, that's fine, dear." The word 'dear' felt foreign but also pleasant.

I gathered my clothes in my arms, walked down the stairs, and grabbed a paper bag from the kitchen, tossing everything inside. I threw a piece of paper on the kitchen counter with a list of three names and phone numbers where my mom might try to reach me.

As I headed towards the front door, I heard my grandfather call out. "Tracy, can you please come in here?" His voice sounded low and strong.

I walked to the doorway of their TV room and saw them sitting next to each other on the ivory loveseat, just as always. "Hey," I tried to say as upbeat as possible. Then Mum-Mum and I exchanged some niceties, and I lied about the last couple of weeks. I never particularly enjoyed lying to my grandparents. It always felt especially dishonorable for some reason.

After a lull, I decided this was a good exit point. I said, "Well, great to see you. I'll see you soon."

But as I turned on my heel to walk out, my grandfather yelled: "Stop!"

I turned back to look at him. He continued, in a quiet, angry voice, eyes looking deep into me: "What are you doing?" he asked. "What are you doing to yourself?"

This question completely threw me off-kilter. "I don't know, Pop-Pop. I don't know. But I'm fine. I'll be okay. I've got this. I'll figure it out." Then I turned to leave, not waiting for his reply.

I wanted to get out of there – I walked straight toward the front door where my mom was standing, holding the door open. I scooped up my paper bag, and looked back at Ruffles who was still sitting by the stairs. Her wagging tail had quieted.

"See ya," I said, looking at her, willing my eyes not to water. I nodded to my mom and headed back down the walkway and around the corner to Mitch's car, engine still running.

I got high, really high that night, trying to forget that painful interaction with my family.

At Mitch's house the next day, his home phone rang. He answered the phone, hesitated, and then called me over. It was my mom. For a moment I was filled with relief that it had worked – seeing me in person had made her want me to come home.

"Hi, Mom," My voice had a little more energy to it.

Silence.

"Mom?"

She inhaled deeply, and with a strained and shaky voice she said to me: "You probably won't make it home before he's dead." And she hung up.

I didn't. I didn't make it home before my grandfather was taken out of the house to the hospital where he died from a brain aneurysm.

I arrived at home where my grandmother had just lost her husband of a thousand years and my mom had lost her dad. I wasn't sure if my presence would add comfort or additional pain, but my mom said I was allowed to stay in the house until after the funeral. I nodded and asked if there was anything I could do to help.

"Maybe just help around the house, help take care of Ruffles. Your grandmother and I will be busy with all the arrangements." Her eyes and lips were swollen from crying.

"Of course, I will." And I did. The next few days were overwhelming, with people coming and going and decisions being made. What am I going to wear, who is going to speak, somebody take care of Mum-Mum, Ruffles is acting weird, we need more food in the house, etc. I snuck out when I had a chance to get high, but I generally tried to keep myself in decent shape.

***

We buried my grandfather on a cold Friday afternoon, February 2nd 1996. The funeral was lovely. I did my duty and stood in line to hug guests, interact with my family members, and cry at appropriate times – but I was actually entirely numb. And by that evening I was back in my room, thankful to be away from all the commotion. But I found myself unable to enjoy the comfort of my room and my bed. Instead, I felt something lurking deep inside me, stalking me. I couldn't quite put my finger on the feeling. Helpless ... empty ... adrift.

I was lost in thought when I suddenly heard my mom calling to me loudly. "Tracy! Tracy! Come downstairs! Please – hurry!"

She was in the kitchen. She was on her knees leaning over Ruffles who was lying on the wooden floor by the island.

"Something's wrong," she was mumbling. "Something's wrong. Something's wrong. What do we do? What do I do!?"

Ruffles' breathing was very labored. She was struggling to stand up and could not. She had wet the floor, and a look of abject fear was in her eyes....

This can't be happening. Not this.

Not this.

On the night of my grandfather's funeral, Ruffles died in our kitchen. At some point my mom finally called our neighbor to take her out of the house. She weighed about

35 pounds and he awkwardly knelt down to scoop her up, not saying a word. She had gone pretty stiff by then and her legs stayed stuck out, her body like a mannequin. My mom opened the garage door and the neighbor walked out with Ruffles.

Mom and I stood side by side in utter silence, caught in the fear that if either of us spoke, it would make this moment real. Tears welled up in my eyes as I stared at the spot where Ruffles died. Where I kissed her and told her not to worry and said goodbye – where I last petted and smelled her soft, wavy, crimped white hair.

I walked over to where she had been lying, and was surprised when I felt her warmth, her beautiful body heat, still present in the hardwood floor. I lay down and balled myself up on my right side and absorbed her heat. I stayed there ... until she was gone.

Two days later my mom told me to pack my bag. I could barely believe it. "I said you could stay through the funeral. The funeral is over. It's time for you to go."

Was she serious?

Silent and in total shock, I walked upstairs and packed my suitcase. What should I do? What could I do? Think!

I saw my mom waiting by the front door as I came downstairs. She opened the door. She was serious.

I was digging deep, trying to muster up the courage to walk out that door, to go figure out my next move. I've got this, right? I've got this! Just keep walking.

I paused at the door. I looked back at the spot next to the stairs for Ruffles. She was not there. She was gone. All I had left of her was our spot on the floor and the memory of her heat.

In that moment, looking at her empty spot, looking at my mom holding the door open to kick me out again, I realized – I couldn't do this anymore.

I fell next to my suitcase, crying, slumped over, almost unable to move. And I found myself saying it out loud, "I can't do this anymore, I can't. I don't know. I can't." I was crying and crying, sharing this sudden confession as my mom leaned over me - hugging me, also crying.

I didn't know what I meant by those words – I didn't know what I wanted to have happen next. Did I want to stop using drugs? Was I done? Did I want to die? Did I want help? Was I really done? I didn't know. I just knew that I was broken. That was the feeling – total brokenness. My soul was broken ... and I had no idea how to fix myself.

After I calmed down a bit, my mom said, "Okay. You can stay. But you must get back into a recovery program."

"I am NOT going back to that place, Mom – it was just too terrible!" I stammered with both anger and fear in my voice.

"Okay, okay," she said, "I will look into other rehab programs close to home. But when I find one, you will start right away – promise?"

I agreed to the deal. But while it was clear to me that my way wasn't working, I still didn't know where to go next. I was in purgatory. I needed a miracle.

IN RETROSPECT

I can tell you every detail of my last interaction with my Pop-Pop. He was seated to the left of my grandmother. His right hand rested on top of her small left hand. He was wearing tan pants, a white shirt, and a V-neck sweater that had navy-blue and maroon stripes in the front. And in his eyes I could see his concern, his worry, his anger – and his love for me.

He was the only father figure who ever stuck around for me, ever gave a shit, ever did anything positive. And I was such a disappointment – such a pathetic disappointment to him. And I will never get that time with him back. I can never show him who I am today and what I've become. This memory still breaks my heart.

I'm so sorry, Pop-Pop. Thank you for taking us into your home when we escaped Richard ... but most of all, thank you for loving me – I didn't deserve it.

And then there's Ruffles. Her death was horrific – but I also think her death is what saved my life. She was the catalyst; her fading heat was a beautiful light going out so that mine could turn on.

Without the deaths of Pop-Pop and Ruffles to shatter me, to make me see my brokenness so clearly, I don't know if I would have sought the help I so badly needed.

|| Send Me an Angel ||

The very next day my mom set out to find me another rehab. Another rehab. Just what every teenager wants – to fail out of one rehab and have to start at another. This was certainly not part of my plan. And as I heard her talking to various people on the phone about my situation, I started to have a sinking feeling that maybe I wasn't fine. Maybe this was bigger than I thought. Maybe (I just might) have a real problem. But was it a problem I was ready to address?

By Tuesday she had found me a place. It was an intensive outpatient program designed for teenagers, located about 15 minutes from our house. I would be interviewed by the counselors on Thursday to see if I was a "good fit," to see if they would accept me for their group program. "What the fuck does that mean?" I thought to myself. "Like, are they going to decide if I'm the right 'junkie for the job'?" Is there even a way to fail this interview? (*Psssst. Yes, there is ... and I almost did.*)

Thursday arrived. I was scheduled to talk to the counselors at 2:00 p.m. I hadn't stopped using completely after my epiphany that Sunday afternoon. After all, I was still a fucking drug addict. But after some convoluted thought, I determined that I shouldn't get high before going in to talk to rehab counselors (a conclusion I hope you've never had to come to yourself). So by the time 2:00

p.m. came around, I was feeling kind of edgy, to put it mildly.

I rolled into my interview entirely uncertain about this next step. Sitting in a sterile room across from these two counselors made me rethink this deal. I knew something had to change – things had clearly gone too far – but deep down, I really had not planned on completely stopping using and drinking. I thought I just needed some time to get my footing and figure out how (or if) I could keep my partying under control.

The conversation/interview with the counselors was tricky. I was no longer in a situation where I could lie about my use. It's hard to convince someone by saying, "Well, sure, I dabble but it's not that bad," after you've already signed yourself out of one rehab. Besides, by this point my mom knew how bad it was, which meant these counselors knew how bad it was, which meant I had to answer most of their questions at least somewhat honestly – and being honest was not a strength of mine at this point. Frankly, it felt like a foreign language. So when asked tough questions, I became extremely standoffish, sarcastic ... a bitchy, know-it-all, messed-up kid.

I don't remember the exact details of the conversation or what went down but I do remember walking out of the room and hearing my mom as she lingered inside to apologize for my tone and behavior toward the counselors – just like I was a fucking toddler (in her defense, I was acting like one).

But by some miracle we got a call the next morning saying that I had been accepted into the intensive outpatient program and I would begin the following week. The group met Monday, Tuesday, Thursday, and Friday from 3:00 to 7:00 p.m. While that sounded like a LOT of time to sit in a group therapy session, at least I wasn't on a plane to Minnesota, so it didn't look so bad in comparison.

Like someone about to go on a diet on Monday, I decided to stuff myself with delicious food – or in this case, various drugs and Icehouse beer – before I would have to starve. I partied hard Friday and Saturday night, and by Sunday morning I felt pretty shitty. I decided not to drink or use that day, Sunday, February 11th, 1996, so that I could pretend to be bright-eyed and bushy-tailed the next day when I started Rehab #2.

On Monday at 3:00, I was sitting across from the two counselors, Jim and Al, in a circle of seven other teens. Everyone went around the room introducing themselves, sharing their name, age, drugs they used, and why they were there. Then it was my turn in the hot seat. Since I was the new kid, I was asked a lot of questions by Jim, Al and several of the other teens.

Jim seemed like a normal guy, in good shape, maybe in his forties. He had an odd sense of calm to him, but he was also funny – like a dry funny. Al was boisterous and colorful. Yes, his personality was colorful, but he was also literally colorful – his clothes were bright mixtures of purple, yellow and orange. He had a raspy voice, funny facial and body expressions, and a very direct energy to him. In hindsight they were an excellent team – balancing each other well, able to play the roles of good cop and bad cop, subtle and direct.

I did my best to beat around the bush to most of the questions, just blowing them off or answering them sarcastically until Al finally addressed me directly: "Honey. What do you plan to do about this?"

"I don't know. I'm here because my mom told me I had to be here in order to stay in the house."

Al followed up: "Okay, but what happens next? Where do we go from here?"

"I don't know. Isn't that your job?" I asked with a smirky smile.

"Ummm-hum. Yes. But what's your role in this? What are *you* going to do?" Al kept at it, leaning forward, elbows resting on his knees while his hands were folded – looking right at me, blinking, lips pursed. Like I was some fucking helpless puppy that he was trying to save.

I raised my voice: "I already told you – I. Don't. Know! Okay? I don't know!" And then for some reason, I started to spew out verbal confession vomit. "I don't know what I'm doing. I don't know what I want. I don't know what's going to happen – I don't know what I even *want* to happen! I just know ... I'm tired. I'm fucking tired! I thought things were fine, or would be fine, but ... they're not. Okay? Things are not fine!"

Jim and Al looked at each other, a bit surprised. I couldn't tell if it was a good surprised or a bad surprised. Then Jim chimed in, "Okay! Thanks for sharing that. So how do you think we could help make things more ... fine?"

"JESUS CHRIST! Aren't you the counselors?" They stared at me. The whole group stared at me. And then I offered up this next statement, one that I immediately regretted.

"How about this? How 'bout I don't drink or drug for 30 days, how does that sound? For 30 days. Huh? And if you don't work some freaking miracle in 30 days, then I'm out of here."

Again, I saw their look of surprise. This time I could tell that it was a good surprise. Jim said, "Yup. I think we can work with that. Al? Thoughts?"

Al was still leaning forward, now with his chin on his fist, he looked like Rodin's 'The Thinker.' After a beat, he sat back and nodded: "Oh yes, honey. This will be fun!" And Al gave me a wink.

Shit.

Shit.

This didn't feel like fun. What, exactly, did I just agree to?

Shit.

Shortly after that, group ended, and day number one of rehab number two was over. I went home, and for some reason, I didn't use that night. I returned the next afternoon. Same situation. The eight addicts and two counselors went round and round.

But by Thursday I was not feeling quite as pleasant. Sorry, let me clarify – I was *never* feeling pleasant to begin with, but by that point I was caught in the very nasty physical agony of going through withdrawal ... again. Round two of withdrawal felt particularly terrible. Maybe it was because I knew what was happening and I knew what was coming. Maybe it was also because I actually *could* have used. Right? Like I could have made a call or snuck out to end this torture – this simultaneous feeling of imploding and exploding, this voice screaming in my head, feelings and memories slowly seeping out. I *could* have gotten some drugs and shut it up – shut everything out – unlike when I was stuck in Minnesota.

But I didn't.

I stuck with it and suffered through it, spending most of the time sitting in my bathtub as my shower ran on me until the water got cold. I found sitting in my bathtub or on the floor of my bathroom to be the most comforting during withdrawal. Sitting, pacing, splashing cold water on my face. Sitting again, pacing again. I went through a couple days like this. And because I felt so sensitive physically, I was also sensitive emotionally. If Jim and Al thought I was bad on Monday and Tuesday, they didn't know what they had coming at them on Thursday and Friday.

On Friday, Jim confronted me: "Tracy. I just want to... check in with you. You seem agitated. Are you sure you haven't had a little drinky-poo or tokey-poo over these last couple of days?" He was specifically saying drinky-poo and tokey-poo a bit sarcastically.

"What?" I screamed back. "Are you kidding me!? I'm dying here because I HAVEN'T had a fucking drinky-poo or tokey-poo – why do you think I feel so fucking terrible?"

"Good to hear," Jim said with a smile, while Al did quiet little claps and added, "Lovely!"

These two ...

I somehow made it through the weekend. I watched more television and movies than I'd ever watched in my life. I made excuses to Mitch and other people about why I couldn't go out that weekend – and when I arrived to rehab that Monday afternoon, I still had not used.

But like before, the drugs were no longer keeping the lid nice and tight on the trash can of my soul, so to speak. Without the drugs I was a walking time bomb, a total train wreck. And I spent the next two weeks in group doing what I had done at rehab number one – goofing off, playing jokes on the counselors, turning the other junkies against them.

In a word, I was pure poison. My insides were rotted, and like a bad strawberry, I wanted to make sure the entire carton turned rotten with me. As the comedian Gary Gulman shares about the dangers of adding grapefruit to a fruit salad: "I am bitter, now everybody's bitter."

I was doing anything to take the focus off the stench of my trash, until finally my obnoxious behavior got me in trouble. I was asked to stay after group on Thursday, February 29th (Yes, I have this correct - it was a Leap Year). Jim and Al wanted to speak with me and my mom. I had become poisonous enough, tainting the rest of the group, to where they wanted to kick me out.

Were they serious? Kick me out? I had done what I said I would do! I hadn't used any drugs – ANY DRUGS – nor had a drink in almost 20 days. I was actually one of the few people in the goddamn group that was *not* using. And they wanted to – let me get this straight – kick ME out?!

As my peers left our Thursday session, a few of them gave me the side-eye, knowing I had been called to the principal's office. My mom entered the room and sat down next to Jim and Al. I felt like I was on trial. I took a seat facing them.

Many words were exchanged between me and them, them and me – and then I was yelling viciously at my mom. I don't recall what exactly I yelled at her but when I did, Al lost it on me. Jumping out of his seat, he knelt in front of my chair and aggressively grabbed both of my shoulders with his hands. He started shaking me and screaming right in my face:

"LISTEN TO ME YOU BITCH! You are going to die! Do you get me? You are going to DIE! You are an ICE QUEEN. You are filled with ice and hate. You have nothing else inside of you. If you don't start to let us in, if you don't start to thaw that ice heart of yours, you are not going to make it! You are going to DIE. Are you listening to me?!"

He was speaking so close to me that I could feel his spit hitting my face as he shouted. Then as he got to the end of his rant, I could see his face softening. He seemed honestly and legitimately scared for me. His eyes were watering and his voice got low and shaky. He barely whispered his final words:

"You are going to die. This *will* kill you."

And then – I'm not sure how to say this – something happened. Something shifted in my universe, and I was blinded by a flash of white light and total silence. While this was probably only one or two actual seconds of time, for me it was as if I got lost in a time warp. I experienced a sudden, distinct moment which filled me with a depth of emotions and a personal awareness – both of which I had been so desperately lacking during my drug and alcohol abuse. It was as if a door, a magical door to my soul was opening and I could see – I could see another side.

I realized that no one out there could help me. This – the substance abuse – this was all my choice and it was my fault that I had ended up here. Yes, I'd been plagued with multiple shitty experiences – my trash can packed full with the abuse of my stepfather, the neglect of my father, and the ripple effects of those experiences on my life. And of course just being a teenager is brutal. But the rest of it – my going numb inside and shutting down my feelings, my progressive plunge into addiction and total spiral downward – that was all me. I felt the weight of guilt and embarrassment for my reckless behavior and actions. But I also felt a wave of humility, clarity, and responsibility wash over me.

In that time warp, within that white light, I felt something snap – and almost instantly I seemed to break free from constantly blaming everyone and everything in the world for my condition. I stopped feeling the intense burden of hate. I stopped hearing that persuading voice in my head encouraging me to use/abuse anything to escape my toxic situation. I stopped seeking numbness.

I again heard that other voice, the one that had spoken to me briefly back in the padded cell in Minnesota – it was true, it was all the things and all my bad decisions – and that blast of insight came through in the flash of white light and silence. If it was ME, if my choices got ME into this mess, then it would be ME making different choices to get ME out of this mess ...

The other three people in that room must have seen the shift in my expression. We all just sat there for a bit, looking at each other, unclear of what to say next. Then Al sat back in his seat, a slight look of uncertainty on his face. "Are you all right, honey?"

I didn't know if I was all right.

I definitely felt different. I didn't react with my usual bitchy defense. Instead, I felt a strange combination of instability ... and faint hope. Tears threatened to flow. Something deep down softened. And then I started speaking, almost not even recognizing my own voice: "I'm sorry, Mom. I shouldn't have said that. That wasn't fair."

I then shifted my focus to Jim and Al. "Look, I know that I suck. I'm not doing well. This isn't easy – every minute is pure hell. But I can see that if I don't work with you guys and get some help, you're right. I'm not going to make it."

They looked at each other, and then Jim took a deep breath. "Okay. Good. We are going to give you one more shot – but hear me, Tracy. You must take the cotton out of your ears and stick it in your mouth. You need to start to listen – because you don't know anything about sobriety."

And so it began. That was the first annoying (but true) recovery quote that I would hear. I would hear many, many more in the following weeks. There would be anthems, mantras, quotes, acronyms, and figures of speech that I would repeat over and over to myself. And little by little, they thankfully started to make sense.

But first I had to take a step – THE First Step. I had to admit that on my own, truthfully, I was powerless over alcohol and drugs. I had to admit to myself and my group and counselor that my life had become unmanageable.

My name is Tracy, and I'm a drug addict and alcoholic.

IN RETROSPECT

I can humbly and fortunately say without pause that Jim and Al were my angels – they were the miracle sent to me.

Months later at a meeting, Jim presented me with his very own 9-month key chain that he had received when he got sober. At that meeting he proudly raised his hand and spoke about the vast change he could already see in me over these past nine months.

In 2007 I got a call that Al had passed away. His lung cancer had returned, but he died peacefully. I had spoken to him two weeks before his death and we'd talked about getting together for dinner. "I love you, honey. I'm so proud of you," I remember him saying before we hung up the phone. A true angel was lost from Earth when Al died.

Jim and I still connect regularly, and on anniversaries I often get a card from him in the mail with a recovery coin taped inside. He's still my angel.

Years after I got sober, Jim and Al told me a story about the first time they met me. They said that Jim hadn't wanted to accept me into the teen rehab program. To him I *had* failed my interview. But Al encouraged him: "Oh, come on, Jim! It'll be fun! We'll try new stuff out on her – see what works and what doesn't." Jim agreed to let me in, but warned Al by saying, "That girl doesn't need a rehab, she needs an exorcism."

And that's exactly what they gave me ...

To my angels, Jim and Al. You saved my life. I love you with all my heart.

ACT FIVE

~~~~~~~~~~~~~~~~

It's the End of the World as We Know It

‖ MEETING MAKERS MAKE IT ‖

"Things break during transformation because they resist."

~ Nate Walker

A NOTE TO THE READER

As you read the stories about my recovery journey, you will see there are a variety of lessons, mantras, and quotes. From the beginning – and throughout my continuous 27 years sober – quotes have been an integral part of my life. They are my source of education, power, and motivation.

I hope you enjoy the lessons and life experiences I share. I hope this information is helpful for yourself and/or someone you love. I hope you, too, find these lessons and quotes inspirational.

I hope.

MY FIRST AA MEETING

The next Monday night after my mind-altering white-light experience, I attended my first AA meeting with Jim. It was a beginner's meeting held in a church about 10 minutes from my house. I'm not sure what I expected – or maybe, WHO I expected – but I was surprised by the people who showed up, and the sheer number of attendees in the room. I watched approximately fifty or so fairly poised people get a cup of coffee or grab a small chocolate chip cookie out of the Entenmanns box, and then stand around chatting with each other before the meeting started. Some were even laughing. Laughing?!

I guess I expected AA meetings to be ... what? Dirtier, darker, sadder? Maybe I expected the people to be a bit more, well, beat-up and desperate? But as I looked around, they weren't. They were, on average, middle-aged happy people who seemed content to be spending an evening at an AA meeting. Weird.

The front of the room had a few long tables making a T-shape, while the rest of the space was filled with rows of metal folding chairs. Jim and I found two seats toward the back on the right side. Someone knocked on one of the tables to quiet the room and the two people sitting behind one of the front tables started talking to kick off the meeting.

Taking it all in, I was a bit lost in thought when Jim gave me a nudge.

"This is where you speak. It's a standard question asked at all meetings to welcome anyone new. You will raise your hand as a new person to AA. Most people say their first name and say they are an alcoholic or addict. You can say both or one – do whatever you choose."

In retrospect, the way Jim handled this situation was brilliant. He didn't give me an option NOT to speak – I *would* be raising my hand – but he gave me the option regarding what I would say. Smart. So, like a good recovery student, I was ready when they asked the question: "Is this anyone's first time at AA? If so, please give us your first name so we can welcome you."

I half raised my hand, certain my face was beet-red. The chairperson (the dude at the long table that kicked off the meeting) pointed to me and said, "Yes, young lady?" And with all eyes on me, I said, "Hi, ummm, I'm Tracy. I'm, I guess I'm an addict?"

I heard a variety of responses to my statement/question. "Welcome, Tracy." "Thanks for coming." "Glad you are here, Tracy!" "Keep coming back!"

Jim gave me another nudge and rewarded me with a nod and a supportive, proud smile.

I sat there for most of the meeting just absorbing it all, observing the order in which things proceeded, curious about the 8x10 framed AA sayings on the walls. I'd heard Jim and Al say some of these before in group: Easy Does It, Live & Let Live, First Things First, Think Think Think, This Too Shall Pass, Keep It Simple, To Thine Own Self Be True – and the big one – One Day at a Time. I wondered, should I take these at face value or is there something I'm missing? Would I soon find myself quoting these?

Surprisingly, the 60-minute meeting went pretty fast. At the end, everyone got up and I just followed the group as they formed a circle around the room and held hands. Okay, I thought to myself, this is getting a little cheesy.

And then everyone started saying something called the Serenity Prayer as we held hands – "God, grant me the serenity to accept the things I cannot change, the courage to change the things I can, and the wisdom to know the difference. God's will, not mine, be done."

Not done yet, the circle of people pumped their still-holding-hands up and down while saying: "Keep coming back, it works if you work it, so work it – you're worth it!"

Ummmmm....

I must admit, the end of the meeting was a little 'kumbaya' for me. And while there was a part of me that wanted to start rolling my eyes a bit at the whole thing – the reading of the 12 steps, sharing the 'tradition of the month,' the cheesy sayings on the walls, the hand-holding thing at the end – another part of me couldn't ignore the fact that I could relate to a lot of the experiences and the feelings shared by these other people of all ages. Shit.

I knew – I KNEW – that I had a problem with drugs and alcohol and that my life had become unmanageable. I knew – I KNEW – like Al had said, that if I didn't stop using and drinking, this festering addiction would kill me. But I also knew I was approximately 20 years younger than every other person in that AA room, and that felt daunting. Would this be my life now? Am I supposed to suddenly catapult from a wild teenager (just approaching my 20th birthday) to a middle-aged sober adult? What about all that stuff in between?

While Jim spoke to a few people he appeared to know, I walked over to the table where they had a bunch of different books and pamphlets displayed. I started talking to a couple of people there who encouraged me to come back or were asking me questions about what brought me to the meeting. At some point I brought up my age.

"I'm nineteen. No offense, but I'm just not sure this is the place for me. I mean, are there other groups? Maybe younger groups? My situation seems a bit different." I thought that sounded nicer than saying, "You are all old as fuck and I am not."

Then a guy, maybe mid-30s, reached over and picked up a pamphlet. He handed it to me and said, "I think they wrote this one juuuuuust for you." And he walked away.

I read the title of the pamphlet: *"Do you think you're different?"*

Touché.

Another nice woman, Melissa – tall, blonde, calming voice – let me know that meetings were held at this location on Mondays, Wednesdays, and Fridays. She said she'd love to see me again, as she patted my arm.

And a crazy thing happened. I did come back that Wednesday, and again that Friday. And then every Monday, Wednesday, and Friday after that for probably the next 3 years.

BABY STEPS

It was a strange time with my mom, Mum-Mum and I living in the house together since we lost Pop-Pop and Ruffles. Their losses were still so fresh, and yet I also felt a sense of newness and hope with each additional day I stayed sober. I could tell that my mom and Mum-Mum were feeling it too, as my interactions with them became more genuine and frequent. We were all experiencing our ups and downs, and I appreciated their smiles and encouragement during this time of mourning.

To stay focused and busy I quickly got a job – two, actually. I opened a fitness center first thing in the morning and worked as a waitress primarily in the afternoons, leaving evenings open for going to AA meetings.

This is what I did day after day, week after week, for months.

Like the framed sayings on the meeting room walls, there were a number of phrases and quotes that I memorized and did my best to live by in early sobriety. But the one that I really latched on to, the one that really worked for me during these early days and months, was "Make the next right decision." It broke down "One day at a time" into bite-size pieces which I needed as a newborn in sobriety. Sometimes I had no idea how to get through one day, but I could definitely try to make the right decisions to get through the next twenty minutes.

In the 1991 movie *"What About Bob?"* there is a fantastic scene where Bob is trying to patiently, uncomfortably wait to receive a phone call. He keeps staring at the clock and repeating to himself: "Baby steps to 4 o'clock. Baby steps to 4 o'clock." And that's pretty much how I spent my first four months of sobriety. Baby steps.

I would make the next right decision to eat a healthy breakfast. I would make the next right decision to show up for work on time. I would make the next right decision to be kind to people when they came in the door. I would make the next right decision to walk straight home after work, not stopping anywhere. I would choose to call someone if I needed support. I would go for a run. I would shower, eat a healthy dinner, and arrive at the meeting on time. I would talk after the meeting openly with people who cared. I would return home, likely watch a movie by myself, and then go to bed. I would do this all again the next day.

Since I didn't know how to function without drugs or alcohol, I became like a horse with blinders on. Don't look left, don't look right – look straight ahead, taking one step at a time. I was baby-stepping. And the crazy thing is... it was working. Sure, I absolutely had passing thoughts about getting high. I missed the numbness pot provided and the ride I got from hallucinogens. But I also knew those things would end me, and I was becoming more interested in where this sobriety thing would take me.

Meetings often included someone reading an excerpt from the Big Book (the 'AA Bible'), reciting part of a chapter called *How It Works*: "Some of us have tried to hold on to our old ideas and the result was nil until we let go absolutely.... Half measures availed us nothing. We stood at the turning point." I connected to this idea that I had a choice. As I had learned from the blast of insight that came through in the flash of white light, I would have to make different choices to get me out of this mess. I would have to 'baby step' forward into a new way of life.

And that's how I looked at each little decision I made – because each seemingly-small decision was a turning point... for better or for worse.

IN RETROSPECT

Twenty-seven years later I am still living by "Make the next right decision." It's so simple – not easy, but simple – and good things seem to happen when I actually practice and live this way. An 'updated' version of this saying is a quote I've come to love (and repeat often, much to the annoyance of my kids). It's by F.M. Alexander: *"People do not decide their future, they decide their habits – and their habits decide their future."*

CHANGE ONE THING --- EVERYTHING

A month into my sobriety, I walked up to the front of that Berwyn Beginners meeting and accepted my '30 days sober' coin. My new AA peers sat beaming at me and clapping. I knew this was something real – this felt good. I wanted more. I also knew that this new life would require me to shed the majority of my old life... And THAT was going to be hard!

Early on I was told about the concept of PPT: "People, Places, and Things." The idea was that you would no longer hang out with the **people** you drank/used with, or people that would trigger you. You no longer went to the **places** where you drank/used, or places that might trigger you. You no longer wore or kept the **things** you had when you drank/used, or kept things that would trigger you. You get the idea ...

"We're only asking you to change one thing, honey. Everything," Al told me with his usual smile and a wink.

"So, you want me to get rid of everything I have and everyone I know? Like, burn down my life? Are you serious? How am I supposed to do that?" I asked.

"Tell me, honey – looking back, how was that life working out for you?"

Yeah, I knew this had to be done. I had been avoiding Mitch, Steve, Adam, and all of my other party friends for weeks, but I couldn't dodge them any longer – and even though ripping off this Band-Aid was going to hurt, I knew life would feel better when it was done.

But remember – baby steps.

I started with Things – that seemed like the easiest of the three. I went through all of my possessions, longingly and lovingly looking at everything – my T-shirts, jewelry, knick-knacks on my counter, music, etc. I put all of my 'trigger items' into two piles: One pile to get rid of, and the other pile – well, I knew they were triggers but I simply could NOT get rid of them, not yet, they held too many memories.

Mostly this latter group consisted of concert T-shirts and cassette tapes. Oh, and a pair of jeans that were Ashley's. They had rips and patches and stained drops of resin on them. These simply couldn't go in the trash. I asked my mom to put all those items in a box somewhere, hoping that one day I could enjoy them again.

I was still avoiding looming confrontations with people, so I made a list of all the Places where I had used drugs – bars and restaurants where I drank, places I would go to sneak a couple hits, even roads I would drive down to get to my dealers. I wrote everything down and shared them out loud with my sponsor. After meeting Melissa at that first AA meeting, I soon asked her to become my 'sponsor' – the person who would walk me through the 12 Steps of AA and basically be my accountability partner and sobriety guide.

I then folded up the piece of paper and put it in my Big Book, inwardly committing to no longer go into or even drive near these places.

Finally: People – this one was the worst. I made a list of all the people I would need to call to tell them I could no longer speak with or see them. I wrote down a paragraph that I would essentially repeat to every person I called. I'd start with the people that I was the least close to, and then work my way down the list.

By the time I got to Steve and Mitch, the calls began to get harder to make. After I read my paragraph to Steve, he was surprisingly accepting – or maybe he was just too high to really respond or care. "Okay, well," he said over the phone, "good luck. Maybe see you around soon." Did he even hear me? Whatever.

Mitch did not respond as well. He got quite defensive and angry. It's of course hard, if you're still using, to have someone go sober – I imagine it can feel like an unspoken judgment. Mitch didn't want to let go of me and our complex relationship. He even showed up at my door at random times or called the house to tell me how this 'sober thing' wouldn't last, that I'd be back. Mitch's determination was actually scary at times. I mean, here was someone actively trying to pull me back into my old addiction mode. But he was also oddly helpful because every time he banged on that door or phoned me, my resolve to stay sober got even stronger.

IN RETROSPECT

I am thankful my mom did not throw out that box of T-shirts and cassette tapes and so forth. I was able to open that box years later with no twinge of a trigger, and to this day I still enjoy those vintage concert shirts. I even have my Motley Crue *Dr. Feelgood* cassette sitting out in our living room, along with our other 1980s memorabilia.

***

I don't know what happened to Mitch, Steve, and Adam. I was creating a new life for myself and they weren't part of it. Even as I got older and technology made it possible for me to 'find' them, why would I? The only thing we had in common I left behind me long ago. I hope they all cleaned up and are safe and well, but that's where it ends for me.

50 DAYS

"Ashley, guess what – it's now 50 days! 50 days! 50 days! Can you believe it? I haven't had any drugs or a drink in 50 days! That's crazy, right?"

Before email or texting or anything electronic, there was good old-fashioned phone calls and writing letters. Though Ashley and I had little correspondence since leaving USC, we still kept in touch from time to time. On this particular day, I remember writing Ashley a letter while sitting on my bed cross-legged, hunching over her green-cushioned tray on my lap – one of the very few trigger items I did not put in the 'things' box my mom had stored away.

I went on writing, telling her about rehab and meetings, working at a local gym and restaurant, how I had gotten back into running and was looking and feeling better than I had ever remembered. I probably wrote three pages in a letter to her, a letter filled with hope and joy. I was so, so proud of those miraculous 50 days. I think part of me wanted her to join me in this journey, but I never said it directly in the letter or on the phone when we spoke.

On the back of the letter where I would seal it, I wrote the number "50" all over. Tracing over the numbers until they were thick and bold.

I missed seeing Ashley – just hanging out, listening to music, and talking about nothing, laughing endlessly. And yet I also struggled with what our friendship might look like now that I was no longer using and drinking. If I saw her again, would we still connect on the same level? How long would we continue to correspond since things were now different – *I* was different?

We lost touch over that first year of my sobriety, and I would eventually stop writing her. But I remember that letter so clearly. I wonder what she thought as she read it.

I wonder how she is today.

DAVE AND THE MALVERN CENTER TEENS

I had maybe two months of sobriety when, on a Friday night at the Berwyn meeting, a kid I recognized rolled in. I had seen him around before at my rehab center (the second rehab). But he was in the adult group, and I remember asking my counselor why this guy, who seemed my age, was in the adult group when I was in the teen group.

Al said, "Well, honey, you're sicker than he is. You need extra hand-holding!" And then Jim and Al laughed and laughed. I'm glad my situation was so hilarious to them...

Anyway, I went up to him after the meeting and introduced myself. It was nice to see a young person attending the group.

"Hey. I'm Dave," he responded easily.

While we were chatting, Dave told me about a young person's group not far from the Berwyn meeting at a place called the Malvern Center. He said there were about six people that regularly attended, all roughly 17 to 25 years old. They would have a meeting tomorrow, Saturday night, at 8:00 p.m. I told him I would be there, excited to meet sober people my age.

Up to this point I hadn't really hung out for fun with anybody. All I did was work, go to my outpatient group, attend meetings, and read, write, or think about recovery. Outside of my part-time gym job, recovery was my real full-time job.

When I arrived at the 'young persons' meeting I was greeted by Dave and a few others. Jay seemed to be the leader of the group, he was few years older, mid-twenties, and had the most sober time, meaning the longest number of consecutive months sober.

There was another guy, also named Jay in the group, younger and energetic. Gary – funny, super smart, sometimes socially awkward. Kathy was a sweet, bubbly girl with wavy blonde hair. Plus Dani – she had long, straight brown hair with an amazing Philly accent. And JP, a short, hilarious guy who I think drank way too much caffeine.

At this particular meeting, 'old' Jay was serving as the Chair of the meeting for that night, and 'young' Jay was the Speaker.

To clarify: every meeting had a Chair – someone had to oversee this group of fuck-ups! The Chair, in charge of the agenda, sat up front, read the standard readings from the AA Big Book, kept track of the time, etc. Meetings also often had a Speaker who would either share their personal addiction/recovery experience or speak on a particular topic for that meeting. Those are the basics you should know – back to the story...

This meeting, however, went a little differently than the standard meetings I had previously attended. I liked how Old Jay didn't exactly follow the agenda or read every word from the Big Book pages. Instead, his approach was: "Okay, welcome – any first-timers? Put money in the basket to support the meeting. Here's the clipboard, sign up to make the coffee or something. Blah, blah, blah..."

And Young Jay was all over the place when sharing his story. He didn't follow the suggested order typically used in AA when sharing a recovery story: "What it was like, what happened, and what it's like now." Instead, he rambled, bounced around, meandered through tangents. It was clear he hadn't shared his story out loud before, or maybe even thought much about it until now.

I appreciated the lack of formality, and I found the meeting entertaining. It was lighter and not as robotic as the ones I had been attending thus far. The rigid structure of AA was something I absolutely knew I needed. But in this space, we were all facing this big challenge and we were also allowed to be stupid kids.

We went out for a pizza and soda after the meeting, and talked late into the night as we sat on the curb outside the just-closed pizza place. That was the latest I had been out since just before I got sober.

My mom was awake, waiting for me when I got in around midnight. You could tell she was worried – worried that I had somehow suddenly slipped and used drugs or alcohol. As I got home, she did that parent thing where she leaned in to give me a kiss, but inhaled through her nose to see what she could smell. She was also looking deep into my eyes to see if they were glassy or if the pupils were enlarged.

"Mom. Please – I wasn't doing anything! I just went to a meeting and actually hung out with some younger sober people afterwards. We had ... fun!"

IN RETROSPECT

I have such fond memories of those meetings and wonderful kids. I don't know if I would have made it without the support of other young people, without the crazy sober fun we got into. Don't get me wrong, we had our drama! We had hookups and breakups. We made bad decisions, even sober. But they never included drinking or drugging ... at least not for most of us.

JANIE

One day, a very pretty girl walked into our young adult Malvern meeting. She was quiet and shy... and pregnant. She had gotten pregnant by her ex-boyfriend while using heroin together. After she found out she was pregnant, she knew she had to stop – and so there she was.

Janie fit into our group nicely, and we all supported her. Dave was probably the most attentive. A few months later he actually started taking Lamaze classes with her to help her when she would have her baby. This was a little hard for me because Dave and I had an on-again off-again kind of crush on each other. Nothing had happened outside of a kiss here and there, but still it was hard for me to watch him dote over Janie. Hard, but at the same time I was touched by how sweet he was to do this.

Months later, she had a healthy baby boy. Janie then decided not to pursue a relationship with Dave, which I could tell really hurt him – he truly cared about her. But she was a new mom to a baby that wasn't his, and she was still new to sobriety with much bigger things to deal with than a casual romance.

Additionally, after the birth of her son, Janie would relapse from time to time, meaning she would go back to drinking or taking drugs. By this point I had seen a number of people raise their hand at meetings to share that they had 'slipped' and were back trying to get sober again with just a handful of days since their last drink or drug. I had not slipped, nor had Dave or some of my other peers, but I did wonder if failure to stay sober was inevitable at some point. Was using again to be expected?

I was genuinely proud of every moment and every win in my sobriety – I *really* didn't want to slip. So as I watched Janie and others relapse, I decided to come up with a pretty solid toolbox containing supportive tips, tricks, strategies, sayings, and anything else helpful to stay sober.

Janie eventually moved farther away with her son to be closer to her mom. We would still see her from time to time and keep in touch.

When I was about six years sober, I got a call from Dave who was crying.

Janie had died from a heroin overdose.

IN RETROSPECT

Janie's death was heartbreaking, her loss felt deeply by our sober friend group (which had dwindled dramatically, as is the nature of relapse and addiction). I recalled the circumstances of her death after I had my daughter in 2008. While holding my baby girl, even with over 12 years sober under my belt at this point, my resolve to stay sober was strengthened as I thought about how Janie's sweet son had lost his mom to drugs.

Dave is still sober today. For over 27+ years, we have experienced ups and downs in our lives. He is an essential part of my consistent recovery. Dave is one of my most trusted best friends. He is the godfather to our youngest daughter. I love you, Dave, and I know I wouldn't be here without your support and humor through the years.

BEHIND THE CURTAIN

In a large meeting one evening, Dave raised his hand to share. He stood up but hesitated before speaking, rubbing his eyes and forehead like he was frustrated. He and I had both been sober for around ten months at this point, and I felt like we were sharing a good groove of working, starting to attend classes, going to meetings, etc. And then he made a comment that I still remember 27 years later:

"Hi, my name is Dave and I'm an alcoholic and addict." (Crowd response: "Hi, Dave!") "You know, I've been coming to these meetings for a decent number of months now, and I hear what you're saying – one day at a time, one day at a time, one day at a time." Again, he hesitated.

"And that's what we're doing, that's what *I'm* doing. But even though you are saying one day at a time, you assholes really mean forever."

His blunt honesty and bold statement had most of the group laughing or nodding their heads in agreement. But hearing this raw truth spoken aloud shook me. It was as if somebody exposed the man behind the curtain, like I was suddenly squinting hard enough to be able to see the puppet strings. It *was* one day at a time ... but for the *rest* of my time.

In my early recovery months and years, I did experience fears regarding how I would celebrate certain milestones in my life – would I drink along with everybody else to celebrate graduating from college? Or at my wedding, would I be able to 'cheers' my new husband without a glass of champagne? What would those experiences be like without alcohol or drugs? What about when I gave birth to my children – would I risk taking painkillers or an epidural? And in general, what about hanging out with friends? Going out to dinner? Vacations? Would I always just order ... water?

Early on, I would think about these multiple future-life events and ponder what they would potentially look, feel, and be like without a drink in hand or hit of a bowl in celebration. But I would push them aside and continue focusing on my recovery and the next right decision one day at a time.

Four years later, as I was approaching my college graduation from Villanova University, I had an epiphany. I realized that graduating from college NEVER would have happened at all if I had had a drink or a joint in celebration of anything. During my addiction, drinking and using was never 'celebration' for me – it was always a necessity, like a thirst that would never be quenched. Any celebration or good thing I hoped for in my future would not happen if I relapsed.

So onward I would go – one day at a time... for the rest of my time.

IN RETROSPECT

For my 18-year sobriety anniversary I was asked to speak at an AA meeting. After the meeting a bunch of us were outside talking and a guy, maybe ten years older than me, said "Wow. 18 years. That's pretty amazing – may I ask, how did you do it?"

In my head I started to go through all the lessons, quotes, tips, and tricks and other things that I've applied in order to get – and stay – sober for 18 years. I was about to rattle all these off, like a list of sober To-Do's – but then I paused.

This was a trick question.

I looked him in the eye and smiled. "One day at a time," I answered simply.

He smiled back at me, nodded, and said: "Good job."

|| GET BUSY LIVING ||

"Get busy living or get busy dying."

~ *The Shawshank Redemption* (1994 movie)

RUN, FOREST, RUN

After a month of sobriety, I became more aware of the idle time I had during the day – and I didn't like it. I thought about what one of the old-timers had told me the week prior. He grabbed me after a meeting and pointed to a sign: "See that sign on the wall? The one that says, 'Think, Think, Think'?"

"Yeah. What about it?" I asked.

"That's not for you. Don't think. Thinking is bad news for you right now." Kind of an asshole comment, I thought, but he also wasn't wrong. I needed to stay busy.

The job I got at a local health club was perfect because they needed somebody who could open up the gym at 6:00 a.m. and stay until about 11:00 a.m. This situation was just what I needed at the time. I would have to go to bed early in order to get up early, and since I was still not allowed to drive my mom's car – "Trust is earned," she would say – I would walk the 1.7 miles to work.

Normally such a morning walk would not be a big deal, but this walk was unfortunately straight up a giant hill. No matter – I would arrive and be greeted by half a dozen members waiting outside at 5:55am for me to open the club so they could get in their workouts before work. This routine kept me very busy – no time to think (or slip).

The bonus of this job was that I started getting back into running. I was actually amazed at how quickly my body seemed to heal from all the damage my drug and alcohol use had caused. I was looking and feeling better every day – my skin, hair, and nails actually appeared to have some moisture. I no longer looked jaundiced. I felt a brightness returning to my face and smile that I hadn't seen in years. After a few weeks of coughing up brownish phlegm, I moved forward, starting to run again several days a week.

For many people, running is like a religion. I got to meet one such person as part of my intensive outpatient rehab program with Al and Jim. By this point, I had done a complete 180-degree turnaround, going from the bad egg in the outpatient group to being a kid who truly cared about sobriety.

On Tuesday evenings we had 'family night,' where the parents would join the kids in a group therapy session. The parents were allowed to voice their concerns and discuss the things they were seeing at home, while Jim and Al would help moderate these often-heated conversations. My mom and I now had much less of this type of tension – instead, in alignment with my abrupt change in the rehab group, our relationship was also encouragingly evolving.

During one of these family meetings, I mentioned my new job at the gym and running on the treadmill after work. One of the parents, named Don, came up to me after the group and started to share about how he was a runner as well. It was a nice conversation that I didn't think anything of at the time, but then at the next parent meeting he approached me and my mom and brought it up again.

"How often do you run? How many miles do you run? How fast do you typically run?" Don asked.

"I don't know, maybe four to five times a week." I answered, wondering why he was asking. "I'm not fast but I can do a decent distance, four or five miles."

"Do you think you could run ten miles?" he asked.

"Like, in one run? I don't know." I kind of laughed. "I'd probably have to walk some of it but yeah, I'd get through it." Again, why was he asking me this?

"Well, I'm signed up for a run that I've done many times," he explained. "It's called the Broad Street Run in Philadelphia. It's 10 miles long and a lot of fun. I think what you're doing and what you've shared in these meetings is tremendous – and I thought you might enjoy setting a new goal. As a runner and a parent, I just wanted to, I don't know, be supportive."

Don looked at my mom. "You must be so proud of her," he said (his son wasn't doing so well).

She replied with a smile, "Absolutely, yes. It's been a miracle."

Don looked back to me. "Think about the race. It isn't until the beginning of May, and they take last-minute entries."

"Okay, thanks."

The next day after work, I decided to run 4.5 miles on the treadmill. And by the time I saw Don again the following Tuesday night, I was up to a somewhat comfortable 5+ miles. And he was right – it was nice to have a goal. Running helped me focus on the next quarter mile, it helped me not to think.

"Okay," I told him, "I'll do it. I can't promise you I will be fast, but I can do the ten miles."

So just a few days before I would achieve 90 days sober, I ran the Broad Street Run with Don by my side, matching my slow jogging pace the entire ten miles. Yes, in hindsight this situation was a little weird – an older man taking a strong interest in this teenager in rehab. But the story ends well – no pervert stuff happened. This was just a good guy trying to share his love of running with a newly sober kid. The world needs more Dons.

And I'm so glad I trusted this man and heeded his advice to set this goal. I would run the Broad Street Run half a dozen more times in the years to come – and I would think of Don each time, wondering how he and his son had made out.

Running and fitness would continue to be an important part of my sobriety and are a huge part of my life to this day. I think Blair Morrison of "Fitness is…" said it best:

"I've heard a million reasons why goals weren't reached or why hurdles were too high. But no justification, no matter how convincing or true, ever transformed failure into success. No task, whatever it may be, will ever make itself easier to overcome because you are tired, sick, or haven't had your coffee. This is fitness' beautiful simplicity. You either lift the weight or you don't. 'Almost' doesn't count."

IN RETROSPECT

This grit (sometimes grind) was taught to me in the rooms of AA. Though discussed here in relation to fitness, I find the process of setting goals to be applicable to anything in life. I wasn't *almost* going to be sober today. I wasn't *almost* going to attend class for school. I wasn't *almost* going to go for that run first thing in the morning. I was going to get up, suit up, and show up. Enjoyment was optional.

Many of the best lessons I've learned, both in recovery and during my 27+ years as a (relatively) mature adult, have been SIMPLE – but simple does not mean EASY. If it was easy, everyone would get sober and not relapse. If it was easy, everyone would exercise daily or lose the weight. If it was easy, everyone would get good grades or be successful or whatever. But if you KISS (*Keep It Simple, Stupid)* and stick with it, change will happen.

TRUST YOUR GUT

I sat inside my car parked on a street near a bar called *The Wild Onion*. I was torn. Though I wanted to see my classmates at this impromptu one-year mini high-school reunion and have a 'normal night out,' I was also struck with two other facts:

1) What exactly would I tell them about my current 'situation?' – and ...

2) Should I really be going into this bar?

Though I was coming up on four months and feeling a level of pride and success in my sobriety, I also felt frozen as I sat there in my car watching my classmates and friends laughing as they entered the bar. I felt embarrassed about my behavior and choices over the previous four years, and I wasn't sure if "Hey, I'm four months sober!" was what I wanted to present to my peers.

As I sat there, hands clenching the steering wheel, I saw my friend Maria from high school standing next to her car talking to someone while smoking a cigarette (or maybe a joint) – and a feeling I wasn't expecting swept over me. I'd assumed my addict brain would reflexively say YES, PLEASE! But instead, I found myself feeling physically repelled, almost like an allergic reaction to something.

Maria finished smoking whatever she was smoking, fluffed her hair, and reapplied her lipstick in the side mirror before heading into the bar. I thought about what it would be like to talk to her at the bar, the smell of beer and liquor in the air, perhaps smelling pot on her breath, looking into her glassy eyes ... and I realized that I simply could not go in. My gut was shouting at me: "This doesn't feel right. Not this time. Not yet."

I started my car, pulled out of the parking space, and drove home.

I learned a valuable lesson that night – I learned to trust my gut, to trust my inner voice that would whisper (sometimes yell) at me over the years. That voice seemed to care and want the best for me. Especially in early sobriety, if a party or situation didn't feel right – for a specific reason or for no reason at all – I would just get up and leave. No rationalizing the gut feeling away because the lurking potential to drink or drug was simply not worth it.

I realized something else that night as I sat there in the car wondering what I would say about my current place in the world to my peers. I recognized it was time to start figuring out my next steps, a plan for the future.

I had left the University of South Carolina after one semester with a 1.4 GPA ... what the fuck was I supposed to do now?

IN RETROSPECT

I'm grateful I did trust my gut and not go into that bar – I wasn't ready. But after more time sober and finding my way, when I did reconnect with my high school friends, I was welcomed back with love and forgiveness. They knew 'something' was going on with me, but never understood how bad things had gotten. To this day, my high school girlfriends are some of my absolute favorite people. I am grateful for these (30-year) friendships.

FIGURE IT OUT

"Commitment is doing the thing you said you were gonna do long after the mood you said it in has left you."

~ Darren Hardy

"Success only comes when you want it bad enough," a man named Bo said to me after a meeting. I had shared my feeling of being stuck in my 'next step' plans. "Don't give me that woe-is-me bullshit," he said to me (he was known for his tough love and direct statements). "Get to work, figure it out!"

Bo used to really piss me off – but he was also right. I would have to be the one to figure it out and it was going to be hard. I knew deep down that I could do it – that I was capable and smart – but I was also still battling the booming voice of my stepfather that remained from those years of him telling me how I didn't know anything, that I would never become anything, that I was a stupid kid.

And as I dug in, as I worked to figure out my next steps, 'The Fighter' was born in me. This internal Fighter was strong and passionate, and even though she had heard the long-ago demeaning words of my stepfather asserting how I'd never amount to anything, the Fighter in me now rose up and shouted back at him with unexpected intensity and conviction: "Watch me."

So I made plans to get myself back on my feet regarding my higher education. I started small (baby steps) ... but dreamt big. I knew I had to improve my GPA for another college or university to even consider me. Proud to see me taking steps forward, my mom and Mum-Mum cheered me on as I started classes at my local community college in the summer of 1996. I took as many prerequisite courses as I could, and I worked hard to get straight A's.

After 18 months of classes at the local community college, I applied to Villanova University, an excellent school not far from my home... and they did not accept me. Though I got a rejection letter in the mail, the Fighter refused to be rejected. She got dressed up, grabbed her application, transcript, and rejection letter, and walked into the admissions building at Villanova.

I told the person at the front desk that I would like to speak to someone about my application – they had made a mistake and that I would, in fact, be attending Villanova University. The assistant behind the desk was so shocked that she actually got me an appointment. Two hours later I was stating my case in front of an admissions person.

I guess she liked my spirit because they reconsidered my application and decided that they would accept me after all – but only part-time. I had to prove myself over the next school year with top grades before I would be admitted full-time. I dug in and disciplined myself, studied like crazy – and the next year I succeeded in becoming a full-time Villanova University student.

With my Fighter in full gear, I graduated *cum laude* in 2000. In the meantime, I had decided to become a psychologist. I had always wanted to be a psychologist (remember Miss Teen USA?) and, almost improbably, here I was advancing toward accomplishing this goal. I chose to move on for further education and was accepted into a graduate program at nearby Temple University, where I would receive my Masters of Education in Counseling Psychology, graduating *summa cum laude*.

During my time at Temple, I discovered that I had an interest in groupthink and business psychology. I decided to round out my education with more business classes and was grateful to be admitted to the Organizational Dynamics program at the University of Pennsylvania.

Why am I listing my credentials, almost bragging? Because I worked my ass off for each of them. I showed up every day, consciously making the next right decision, staying sober one day at a time – and yeah, I showed that motherfucker Richard that I was a smart kid.

I AM a smart kid.

IN RETROSPECT

The essay I had to write as part of my Villanova entrance application was titled: 'Who is the most influential person in your life?' And the first line I wrote in response was:

'The most influential person in my life was my stepfather, and may he burn in Hell.'

Hummmm. Upon reflection, maybe this had something to do with that initial rejection. Maybe...

|| I WANT MY BABY-BACK RIBS... AND COLLEGE DEGREE ||

"Every goal you want to achieve is on the other side of a brave decision."

~ Jon Acuff

For three years I lived in Villanova classrooms, the Chili's dining room, and (occasionally, when sleep called) in my one-bedroom apartment where I lived alone. Being busy was a good thing for me. Since 'Think, Think, Think' was supposedly not for me, it made me focus on 'Do, Do, Do.'

During what little free time I had I would usually attend three to four AA meetings a week, exercise, and hang out with recovery friends or whomever my boyfriend was at the time. And while my grandfather had left me some money to pay for my education, I would have to offset those costs and make additional money if I was to avoid school loans. Hence, Chili's.

THE POWER OF A NOD (AND A SHOWER)

I was 22 years old trying to navigate college responsibilities and social engagements as a sober young adult while holding down a pretty busy schedule as a waitress at Chili's. I was cheerful and engaging with a cute swinging blonde ponytail – and it didn't take me long to realize that I was able to use some of the manipulation techniques mastered in my addiction years to upsell every food or drink item possible. At the time I did not realize that many of the lessons I learned at Chili's would be applicable as I advanced in my business career a few years later.

"I'd like a Budweiser please," the guest would ask.

"24 oz, right?" I'd ask with confidence and a nod, not giving them the 16 oz drink option.

And while taking an order I'd ask – always nodding and maintaining direct eye-contact – "Chips and salsa to start off, yes?" Tell *them* what they want.

During the lunch shift, I observed a pattern and found ways to make these few busy hours work to my advantage. I knew that the checks – therefore tips – would be lower at lunch, so my goal was to turn over as many tables as fast as possible. I would take the orders and quickly circle back, dropping off two of each drink (no point wasting time to get them a refill), drop the food, then drop the bill (lunch diners rarely ordered coffee or dessert). I'd have them out of that table in no time – ready for my next victim (customer).

The money was great, but there was a downside to living at Chili's ... the smell.

Because I would often be running either to or from a shift at Chili's, I made a regular habit of changing in the parking lot at Villanova before going into my class. I had a bag packed with a fresh shirt and my favorite hat with me at all times – a light blue hat from Gap with the letters "G A P" in black with a white outline. I wore this hat practically every day to cover my 'smells like fajitas' unwashed hair.

One day I headed to campus early, freshly showered with no Chili's shift scheduled that day. I ran into one of my professors and had a question for her. But when I went over to her and started talking, it was obvious by the look on her face she didn't know who I was.

"Professor Campbell, it's me, Tracy ... from English."

I could see the recognition cross her face as she smiled and responded, "Oh, Tracy, I didn't recognize you without your hat!"

Okay, it was official. I was going to have to find a way to ditch the fajita hair and hat, and find time to shower regularly. Basic hygiene would have to become just as important as grades, sobriety, and earning a living.

IN RETROSPECT

To this day I still use my Chili's techniques in business – the smile, confidence, nod, direct eye-contact, "If you don't ask the answer is always no" mentality. And it was fun to pass them on to my oldest daughter as she got her first job in a restaurant this past summer.

***

Alas, I am still known for my unbelievable laziness when it comes to showering. Between the shampoo and conditioner and brushing it – UGH – it just takes so long! And aren't I planning to work out again tomorrow anyway? "Hey Google – how many days in a row can someone use dry shampoo?" (Asking for a friend.)

THE POWER OF A SIMPLE HELLO

I may have been sober, but sitting in an 8:00 a.m. 'statistics and psychology' class was no picnic for me either. That said, it was probably much easier for me than for the students in the class who were NOT sober.

I found that I learned best by sitting in the front of the class to minimize distractions. Additionally, I sat close to the teacher because I am partially deaf in my left ear (likely thanks to blasting Motley Crue). Because of these facts and my eagerness to get good grades, my back was pretty much toward the entire class. Most of them usually sat in the last two rows while rubbing the sleep out of their eyes for the first hour. I didn't know anyone in the class particularly well, but I did spend two mornings a week with them for a few months, so I would certainly recognize a classmate on campus. And that's exactly what made this next situation so complex.

I was sitting in an AA meeting I had attended regularly on Thursday evenings, just off-campus from Villanova but within walking distance. The meeting had been underway for a few minutes when a guy walked through the double doors. This guy was from my 8:00 a.m. psych class.

I started to wonder why he was there – was he at the meeting for a class? Some psychology and sociology classes required students to attend an AA or NA (Narcotics Anonymous) meeting. Was he there supporting the person he just sat next to? They seemed to nod at each other. Or was he there because he *needed* to be in an AA meeting? I didn't know which question or answer I hoped for the most.

When he finally scanned the room and saw me, his face went white. I could tell the same questions started to race through his head.

"Well, here we go," I thought to myself as I approached him after the meeting ended. Multiple people had been going up to talk to him since he was a new face at this meeting. Because recovery had taught me, "Don't put off tomorrow what you can do today," I knew I had to rip off the Band-Aid and go talk to him before seeing him in our next class. So I waited for an opportunity to introduce myself.

"Hi, I'm Tracy. I know you from our 8:00 a.m. psych class."

"Yeah, I know who you are. I'm Brian," he said with a small smile, chin down, hands fidgeting.

"So – come here often?" I said with an extra-large fake smile. We both laughed and it broke the tension a bit.

"No, not exactly. Ummmm – I've been to a few meetings, but this is my first time here."

"Oh, well, welcome! Good for you. I'm glad you came." He didn't say anything, so I continued. "If it makes you feel any better, everybody here has also experienced that awkward 'first time at a new meeting' feeling."

"So, you come to these meetings, like, a lot?" Brian asked.

"Yeah, I come to this one every week, and usually a couple others during the week at different places. Depends on school and work."

Brian started to relax a little. "Oh, okay. So, how long have you been, like, going to these meetings?"

"Well, I just celebrated two years in February." I knew what was coming ...

"TWO YEARS – holy shit! You haven't had a drink in two years?"

"Yep. No drinks or drugs. I really sucked at it." I chuckled.

"Oh, wait, so THAT'S why you are always so talkative in class! I've got to say, I sit in the back of class and wonder what the fuck kind of coffee you're drinking." Now we were both laughing.

I scrunched up my nose and asked, "Sorry – am I really that annoying?"

"Yeah, you kind of are."

And with that, Brian and I were off to a beautiful friendship. We would be friends through the rest of school and graduate together. He would stand by me and stick up for me when I went through a nasty breakup with someone else in AA.

I'm so glad I didn't avoid him out of embarrassment at that meeting. Through my years in AA I have learned to face uncomfortable things head-on – something beautiful might be around the corner – and to never fear doing the right thing.

IN RETROSPECT – from Brian...

Before publishing, I let my friend Brian read this story. He told me there was so much more to this moment than I had captured. So, I asked him to share his account of our first meeting. Here is what he said:

When I read my beautiful friend's recollection of our meeting – 25 years seeming but a moment ago – I smile. I smile because I know sometimes a "Hello" is just a "Hello." But sometimes "Hello" can be so much more. It can be pivotal. It can be EVERYTHING. It was to me.

Spring semester of 1998. I can still close my eyes and picture her sitting in the front of that psychology class like a tool. And with warmth in my heart, I will tell you that I DID find her to be annoying all semester. And it had nothing to do with her peppy good looks, her charismatic exuberance and cheerfulness, or the sitting in the front row always raising her hand. When one is either drunk from the night before, hungover, or just passively suicidal as I often was, everyone is annoying. This Main Line Barbie was my antithesis – a vibrant reminder that I was so truly and desperately lost – struggling with an addiction that I didn't realize that I had and the unshakeable darkness fostered by it. "What the fuck is her deal?" I would often wonder. I would soon find out.

The night we met I was within my first 30 days of sobriety, still completely lost and looking for answers. I was teetering, unsure that I could swallow all that these AA fucks were peddling, unsure if I wanted to continue with sobriety. Desperation had driven me to this meeting on school grounds, probably one I would never have attended for fear of being discovered. And when I walked into that meeting, the last person on the planet that I would have ever expected to see was there – the annoying girl from psychology class, sitting in her trademark front row seat!

I don't remember a single word shared at that meeting. What I remember is that SHE was there, that she introduced herself to me after the meeting, and that she was over 2 years sober - which was a fucking eternity to my 21-year-old self. She talked with me long into the night on the sidewalk outside of that meeting, long after everyone else had left. That lingering "What the fuck is her deal?" question that I had been asking myself all semester had been answered – it now made perfect sense.

Lighthouses were built so that ships in the night could safely navigate their way to shore without getting lost or smashed into the rocks. This beautiful, happy, vibrant, energetic spirit had been showing me all semester where sobriety leads - both before and after I got sober. All my doubts about what I was doing, where I belonged, and where I was going had vanished. Tracy has always been and will always be my lighthouse. People like myself, those with a darker disposition and who naturally find comfort in the shadows, absolutely need them. We are hopelessly lost in a sea of darkness without one. I would not have gotten to 25 years of consistent sobriety without her light.

When I truly consider my mental state at the time we met in conjunction with how explosively violent and self-destructive my drinking was, it is not a stretch to say that my amazing friend probably saved my life. THAT is the power of "Hello."

I will forever be grateful to and appreciative of her – and whenever I see a lighthouse on the California coast, I smile and think of her to this very day.

Thank you, Tracy.

THE POWER OF CONVICTION

In order to graduate in the Spring of 2000 I had to take a variety of summer classes to catch up on credits at Villanova. Between my junior and senior year, I took a sociology class over the summer where the majority of our final grade for the class was determined by a group project with teams assigned by the teacher. Our group had five people, and after the first meeting it was obvious that I would be the leader. Two of my four partners were (thankfully) interested and invested in the project, one wasn't particularly motivated, and the other one... well, he didn't even show for our first meeting. But I wasn't about to let a group project bring down my GPA – I would need to take the reins.

We discussed who would complete which sections of the report, and what the timing and expectations were. We would meet four more times over those four weeks, the original 'no-show' only attending one of those meetings (grossly unprepared). It was clear that myself and the other members of the group would have to write his section of the report. Since he was a prized basketball player for Villanova University, he didn't seem to care about his grade – and I'm pretty sure he didn't exactly need to care. Basketball was kind of a big deal at Nova, and it wasn't like they were going to kick a basketball player off of the team for a C in summer sociology.

During our final class at the end of the month we had to turn in our final report to the teacher. I had compiled all of our group's work – including the work I did for the asshole hoops star – and with a sigh of relief I dropped the thick stack of papers on the teacher's desk.

As I was walking back to my seat, the teacher said: "Excuse me, but I think you are missing a name on your paper."

I turned to the teacher and said with a pleasant smile, "No, those are the people who participated in the report."

"But there were five people in your group, and I don't see Ben's name on the paper."

I had been hoping he wouldn't notice this omission during class, and that he might have to use this new 'e-mail' thing or follow up with me about it at a later time. But nope – it looked like we were going to do this now. In class.

"Well," I hesitated, gathering the courage to say what I was about to say. "Since he didn't participate in our group, I didn't put his name on our paper."

Ben, gracing us with his presence for this final class, chimed in, "What? Are you serious?" (I'm pretty sure we all heard the word 'bitch' whispered under his breath.).

The teacher continued: "I see. But he was assigned to your group, so I'll need you to put his name on the paper."

Gulp... I persisted. "He may have been assigned to the group, but he didn't do anything. I – we – wrote his part of the paper. He wasn't an active part of our group."

"Yes, Tracy, noted. But please just write his name down – here." He pushed the paper toward me on the desk. The entire class was silent. They looked from the teacher to me, back to the teacher, back to me like a tennis match.

Deep inhale. "I cannot write his name on this paper in good conscience. If you feel the need to add his name to that paper, then you can write it on the page yourself. I am not going to be adding it."

The teacher had a pretty stunned look on his face, and he was silent for a moment. The class responded with oohs and ahhs. And by this point, Ben's expletives were pretty loud.

I just nodded, then walked back to my desk and sat down. Of course, I was worried about how my dissension was going to be received by the teacher and how it might even affect my grade. But in the words of *Billie Jean* (1985 movie), "Fair is fair!" – Ben didn't do shit, and he didn't deserve his name on that paper.

And ... a couple of weeks later I received my grade. I got an A in the class.

Fast forward a few months into the Fall of my senior year when one of my teachers recommended I apply for Who's Who of Villanova University. Who's Who is a nationally recognized award, generally given to outstanding seniors who are selected based on leadership ability displayed in the areas of scholastic aptitude, community service, and extracurricular activities. I was honored that my teacher had mentioned it to me and decided to check it out.

As I was reading through the information and application procedures and requirements, I saw a list of the eight Villanova professors who would be reviewing these applications and judging which students would win. One of the names on that list was my sociology teacher from the summer. Shit – not ideal. But I decided to go for it anyway. What did I have to lose?

A couple of months later I was excited to be notified that I would be inducted as a Who's Who member for Villanova University. There would be a dinner honoring us toward the end of the school year. I attended that dinner with my mom, who was so proud to see me receive this reward. At the dinner, I was a bit surprised when my sociology teacher came up to me and shook my hand. He said, "As soon as I saw your name on that application, I knew you would be one of the students I'd vote for."

Recovery provided me with a sense of purpose, a sense of right and wrong, and a deeper knowledge of – and confidence in – myself.

All I can say is – I'm thankful. I like this person.

|| NO ONE CARES... AND THAT'S A GOOD THING ||

I graduated from Villanova University in the Spring of 2000 and went straight to Temple University that fall for my Masters in Counseling Psychology. I quickly realized it was no joke – this program and these people were smart and serious. I would have to stay focused and dedicated, with a clear combination of grit and grind for two years. I learned a lot at Temple from my professors and peers, but there was one particular life-altering moment that stands out.

It was the end of my first year at Temple, and everything was riding on the 15-minute presentation I was about to give to my class. We'd been working on our assigned topics throughout the entire semester, and 50% of my grade would be based on my lecture.

I had endlessly reviewed my speech to where I practically knew it all by heart. That way I would be able to make eye contact with the audience and not just read the report. I had chosen my images and slides wisely, and they were cued up on the computer, which was displaying them on the large screen in the auditorium. I had picked out a professional outfit to wear and was ready to kick this presentation's ass!

They finally called my name – I was very prepared but also (obviously) very nervous. I readied myself behind the podium, nodded to my teacher that I was set to begin, and started in on my presentation.

It was going great! The clarity and projection of my voice was strong, I was able to look at the audience, I was remembering to advance my slides so they fit with the information I was presenting – nailing it!

And then I fucked up.

I was so busy looking out toward my classmates, pretending to make eye contact, showing how I was 'so prepared,' that I mistakenly skipped over an entire chunk of material. In addition to the chunk of material, there was also the accompanying slide. How was I going to skip it? How could I circle back? How could I make this look like I had not totally messed up?

All of this swirled in my head for what felt like forever – and as I reeled in fear, worrying about my classmates' responses to my mistake and my teacher's analysis of my error, blood filling my cheeks with embarrassment, I finally did make *genuine* eye contact with the audience to try to read the room to figure out my next step ...

And do you know what I saw?

Nothing.

No eyes. No one looking at me. No one actually listening to me. They were all looking down at their laps, maybe reading a book, maybe reviewing their material, maybe scrolling through those new cell phone things everyone seemed to be getting. Maybe some of them were even ... sleeping? This went for my teacher as well! He too was looking down at his clipboard, pen in hand, presumably taking notes about my presentation – but he wasn't *looking* at me.

I quickly realized that nobody knew my topic or what I may or may not have covered. If I was to double click and simply jump over the next slide, if I was to just continue with my speech, confidence in my voice like nothing out of the ordinary had happened – maybe no one would even notice my error, including my teacher.

So I continued on as if nothing had happened, successfully completing my presentation. I thanked everyone for listening, stepped down from the podium, and went back to my seat to watch my other classmates present. And guess what happened …

While sitting there, I also found myself not really paying attention to them. I was enjoying the relief of finishing my report and essentially being done with this class. I found myself jotting down my "To Do List" on a piece of scrap paper while my peers lectured about their topic. I realized that, if I was being honest with myself, I didn't really care how my classmates were doing as they presented their lesson. I mean, I wanted them to do well – I'm not an asshole – but at the end of the day I didn't *really* care. It wasn't like I would be thinking or talking about them later that day.

Wait. Was this the way they also felt about me? And like a bolt of lightning, I realized … nobody cared.

From that moment on I began to operate under the assumption that no one cared, no one was really paying attention to *me* – and I haven't turned back since (much to the occasional embarrassment of my husband and kids).

Listen, I understand that some might take this as a negative or disappointing insight – but let me help explain why this is actually a very liberating realization.

For example, think about the last party you went to. You chose something specific to wear. You likely had conversations where you shared your experience or opinions, maybe tried to be funny. You probably ate certain foods and then chatted with people while wondering if something might be stuck in your teeth. Then you likely went home and thought these other people were spending some amount of their personal time and energy thinking about – maybe even talking about – you. But I promise this is not the case. Just as you went home thinking about *you* and wondering what other people thought of *you*, everyone else did the exact same thing.

What does this mean and why is this (mostly) a good thing?

If everybody is almost always thinking about and generally focused on themselves, that means they are not worrying about, thinking about, talking about, or judging you – and that means that you get to just be ... YOU! Wear what makes you feel amazing, share your thoughts and opinions, eat whatever the hell you want, and strut around that goddamn party like the magical person you are, because no one is going home to worry, think, or talk about you. Stop stressing, stop playing games – and just be your true self.

As the saying goes: *"Dance like nobody is watching."* Because really … they're not … and that's a good thing.

IN RETROSPECT

I want to be clear that there is a difference between not worrying about what others think of you and being an asshole. Not caring what other people think doesn't give you the right to be cruel. My hope is that this is a simple invitation to let go of petty worries and embrace a greater freedom to be your beautiful and unique self.

Yes, dance like no one is watching – AND – also be a good and kind human when no one is watching. You can do both.

|| PLANS CHANGE ||

"Every action you take is a vote for the type of person you wish to become."

~ James Clear

Before I started at the University of Pennsylvania in Organizational Dynamics, I decided to take a corporate job. Since I had shifted my plans a bit and wanted to move into business psychology, I thought it wise to devote some time to actually working in a corporate environment. Experience is the best lesson!

A friend of mine told me about a job opening at a healthcare company he had worked with in the past and thought my counseling skills could be useful in this 'market research moderator' role. My friend explained that as a 'moderator,' I would be asking doctors questions to find out information that pharmaceutical companies wanted to know. And with that little bit in mind, I did the best I could at preparing for this interview with no medical or pharmaceutical experience. I would have to go into this conversation with confidence and curiosity while highlighting my counseling and interviewing skills.

That kind of poise and certainty was something I learned as I progressed in my recovery. Little by little, as I glued my fragmented pieces together and came into my own, I liked what I saw – and I hoped this company did too...

I'm happy to say that I got the job! I planned on working full-time while attending Penn part-time for classes. This job would require a lot of travel, which I was excited about, but I also knew I would have to balance it with my classes and schoolwork.

It didn't take long for me to realize that I loved moderating more than I loved working towards another master's degree. I had found a job that was unique, exciting and interesting, a job I excelled at by using all my counseling techniques during interviews ... and it paid well. I decided to end my time at Penn, pursue pharmaceutical moderating – and within four years I had started my own market-research consulting company.

When I was newly sober it was important for me to speak up regarding my concerns, needs and expectations. And as I progressed in my career, I was able to apply that skill as it related to business. *"In business you don't get what you deserve – you get what you negotiate."* (Chester Karrass) And from Nora Roberts: *"If you don't ask, the answer is always no."* By using my voice and valuing my worth, I'm grateful and proud that twenty years later, my consulting company is still successful today.

Another skill I learned early on in this journey and apply to my business (and life) is honesty. I know that sounds trite, but for a skilled addict, liar, and manipulator, fierce honesty was something I had to practice. And after a number of years, recovery has made me a terrible liar – I cannot hold something within me that is untrue.

I remember one scenario with a client about three years into my moderating career. It was an intense, month-long, two-phase project that essentially ended with bad news. My boss and I would have to tell the client that their product was going to receive very little use, probably coming in as a fourth- or fifth-line product, only used after other treatments had failed. I began writing up the presentation, trying to balance kindness with directness while stating the data and quotes from the interviewed physicians to back our findings. My boss, however, wanted to 'spin the results' a bit and go easy on communicating the truth. That's not how I operate, so I let my boss know that he could present the results.

I sat silently (and uncomfortably) as my boss communicated the information. Our main client seemed pleased, but her manager must have noticed my discomfort. Since I had been the one to actually complete all the physician interviews, he asked me to provide my opinion of the project results. I shared my viewpoint and, needless to say, our primary client's smile turned into a frown ... and a couple weeks later we were not asked to bid on the third phase of the project. That was ok with me – most clients appreciate the truth when making multi-million-dollar decisions, and I prefer to not work again with those who only want sunshine and rainbows. Sorry – that's not life, and I'm only serving reality.

A few years after this experience I ran into the manager who had asked me to share my opinion. By that time, he was working for a different pharma company – and he quickly hired me as the main consultant for their qualitative market-research work.

If I'm being totally honest, my Type A personality hates it – hates it! – when plans change. Much like Hannibal from The A-Team, *"I love it when a plan comes together."*

But I've come to believe and trust that there's a bigger plan ... and it's usually better than mine.

ACT SIX

~~~~~~~~~~~~~~~~~

I'm Still Standing

|| THE MANY AND THE ONE ||

It should be obvious by now that there were many, many rules I chose to follow diligently as part of my recovery. I did not, however, heed the standard recommendation that I should avoid new relationships in early sobriety. And while I am grateful and lucky that my relationship choices didn't lead me back to alcohol or drugs, in retrospect it probably would have been best to have sorted through some of my shit before I grabbed onto the next lifeline.

I dated people where I worked, and sometimes they would overlap. Awkward.

I dated people from AA. They too, overlapped. Double awkward.

If I'm being totally honest with myself – and you – I feel like my first five to six years of recovery embodied the quote from Mission Impossible 2: *"You know women, mate. Like monkeys, they are. Won't let go of one branch until they've got a grip on the next!"*

I'm not proud of my continuous cycle of boyfriends. I'm not proud of how I ended some of those relationships, or how I began them, for that matter. I genuinely loved a few of those men, but I still had deeper work and healing to do...

In late 2002, while working and attending Penn, I met a guy who really threw me for a loop. He would push and pull and push and pull on my heart and our relationship. I finally started to ask myself – Why do I keep going back? Why do I put up with him? Why do I feel like I need to 'win' him or hold his attention?

I started to believe that my relationship roller coasters might be related to my flawed childhood father figures. By this point, at over 6 years sober, I sincerely believed I had fought the demons from my stepfather and won. I believed the Fighter was victorious in her many successes, proving him wrong. Yet upon closer review, it wasn't my stepfather that I needed to address – it was my relationship with my dad. But how do you address a relationship where there is none? I had absolutely no idea where to start. And it became clear to me that I would need some serious, no-joke, next-level therapy if I was to ever attain and sustain a long-term healthy relationship with a man.

My mom helped me to get the name of a local psychoanalyst who was supposed to work magic. I met with him quite early one morning before having to drive to work and I explained my situation. He believed he could help, but it would cost me.

"You know, my hourly fee is quite high. I can try to work with you on payment, but is this something you feel you can afford over time?" Dr. S candidly asked.

I thought about this for a moment and then responded. "Yes, I understand – and I'll make it work. Besides, your hourly rate is cheaper than a divorce lawyer ... and if I don't figure this out, that's probably where I'm headed in my future."

He smiled at me, and we scheduled two sessions a week for the next month. "Jesus!" I thought to myself, "this is going to be worse than working out with a personal trainer!"

We immediately started to dig in on the details of my non-existent relationship with my dad. What was it about him – or my reaction to him – that was causing me to choose men who were damaged, closed off, usually needing to be 'fixed' or 'saved' in some way?

As we spent time talking through my memories, thoughts and feelings on this topic, Dr. S let me know that he would also assign me homework. Perfect, I thought, I'm good at homework. I'm a 'Do-er.' Then he told me what the homework would be ...

I was instructed to go see my dad as often as possible, maybe even a couple times a month. This was wayyyyyy more than my usual twice-a-year visits during summer and Christmas.

"What the hell am I supposed to do with him?" I asked Dr. S, slightly irritated.

"Anything. Or nothing," he replied. "You just need to see him and sit with him."

I felt slightly confused about my homework. "But – we don't exactly have a relationship. We have nothing to talk about ... Let me make sure I understand – I am supposed to drive an hour and a half to his cabin to just to ... see him?"

Dr. S nodded. "Exactly. I don't care if your visit is 15 minutes or 2 hours. Just go be with him. Maybe pick up a couple of sandwiches or rent a movie and go sit and watch it with him."

"This homework sucks!" I thought to myself. It was not complicated, it was so simple ... but so unbelievably difficult and uncomfortable. It reminded me a lot of the work I had to do in early sobriety – work that was very effective and successful. So I decided I was going to do it – all in. Besides, I was paying this guy a lot of money, so I'd better heed his advice.

I started to visit my dad whenever I could. Most of the time I would bring him lunch or food to make dinner and we would eat together and watch TV. Sometimes we would go for a walk around his property. He lived on a lovely bluff by a river just off the Chesapeake with its own little private beach and dock. When the weather was nice, we would sit on folding chairs on that dock and gaze out at the water, often not saying anything. It was beautiful. Then I would kiss his cheek and say, "Bye, Daddy. See you soon." And he would reply, "Right, Peach."

He never asked why I was coming to his cabin more often, though I imagine he had to wonder what may have prompted the change. Yet despite his silence on the matter, I could tell that he appreciated my simple drop-ins – our time together felt easier and less forced. I knew he enjoyed our visits... though he could never express it.

This went on for months – and over time, something amazing happened. I stopped having expectations about what our relationship should look like or feel like. I stopped being disappointed and I started to accept my dad for exactly who he was and what he could (and could not) provide for me emotionally.

Instead, I felt a warm peace growing between us. I was coming out on the other side of this pained relationship with some new, essential strength. A depth of acknowledgment, awareness, forgiveness. Yes, I could feel sad at times – but I was no longer feeling broken.

Soon after this realization, around Thanksgiving 2003, I found myself in a situation where I would be able to act on my new awareness. There was a guy I had been dating who was hot and fun, but he often caused complications in our relationship. He'd then have to apologize for messing up in one way or another – and I would inevitably take him back.

My awakening with my father enabled me to see more clearly that I was repeating these old unhealthy patterns – trying to 'keep' or 'fix' him – and I was done playing that game. I broke up with the guy and moved forward in the world with a new sense of groundedness. Relationships would now be on my terms – no more games. No more 'fixing.'

A couple weeks later my (very social) gym hosted a holiday party. A trainer I knew told me about a guy he was working out with – he thought we would be a good fit and my trainer friend wanted to introduce us at the party. I let him know I was quite comfortable being solo and not interested in a relationship ... but I didn't want to be rude, so I said I'd at least meet the guy.

When I was introduced to Mike, it wasn't hard to notice how attractive he was and that he was obviously in excellent shape. I remember the tight blue button-down shirt he was wearing, fitting nicely across his chest and biceps. At some point during our chit-chat I quoted a line from a movie – and he quoted the next line right back. As an avid fan of quotes, I found this to be impressive. I was enjoying talking casually with him, without any games or expectations. I hadn't planned on us connecting after the party, but we did exchange numbers before I left.

We connected a few times on the phone and emailed over the next couple of weeks while I traveled a bunch for work. Having been so used to shallow relationship games, I was pleasantly surprised that it was easy for me to be totally authentic when corresponding with Mike. We decided to get together for a simple pizza lunch – if things didn't click, it was no big loss. I remember thinking, "Gosh, I kinda hope I actually like this guy." He was great on paper – had gone to a good school, had a good job, nice relationship with his family – and obviously attractive. All great qualities, but I was hoping I would enjoy hanging out with him one-on-one.

"No games, no expectations" I said to myself in the mirror before going out to lunch with Mike. And from the very beginning, I was able to be my genuine, silly, assertive, direct self. We clicked – quickly! In honest truth, after just our third date I knew with absolute certainty that I was going to marry him. (Obviously I did not tell him this ... because that would have sounded crazy!)

One month later, during a trip to New York City for the weekend, we were laughing about something when he suddenly paused and got a quite serious expression on his face. He looked me straight in the eyes and said, "I'm in love with you and I'm going to marry you."

With a calm smile, I teased him, "What took you so long?"

We were married 16 months later. No games, no baggage, just a solid, amazing marriage now for over 18 years. I would not have chosen this man if I wasn't sober or if I hadn't worked down into the deepest part of my core to heal my relationship with my dad. I am grateful for my clear head, and for the time and work I put in on myself over the years – I am beyond reaping the rewards!

To Mike, my favorite person ... my cup runneth over. As our song so perfectly states:

> *"There's never a wish better than this,*
> *When you only got a hundred years to live."*

> ~ 100 Years, Five for Fighting

|| MARRIED... WITH CHILDREN... SOBER ||

FAMILY OF FOUR

Mike and I stood in the doorway of the kitchen. I was leaning against the door frame when I saw him simply hold out his fist and look at me. I, too, responded by holding up my fist.

"ROCK – PAPER – SCISSORS – *SHOOT!* "

I lost. And this one was a biggie.

Statistically speaking, while I won the majority of our Rock-Paper-Scissors faceoffs, Mike had a tendency to win the 'big' ones.

We had just spent the past month having conversations here and there about one particular topic. Some conversations were more casual while others were more heated. They were never particularly argumentative and were often very factual, rational. The Topic? If and when to have children.

When I was little, I imagined I would have children in my adult life ... but I started to second-guess that assumption after recovering from my own difficult childhood and all the bullshit that had entailed. I was also, at this point in my life, entirely fulfilled – succeeding in my work and madly in love with Mike – so I was not sure if I needed (or wanted) another human in my life. Mike DID want children, and since I was a few years older than him, he wanted them to come sooner rather than later...

Finally, when this crucial decision came to an impasse, when we had both put all of our cards on the table and made equally excellent arguments in each direction, we realized what had to be done – we would resolve this the way we resolved most things: Rock-Paper-Scissors.

I watched as his paper covered my rock – and right then I realized our lives were going to change forever. We smiled at each other, and we adhered to our rules – the winner does not gloat, and the loser cannot complain.

Three months later I was pregnant. I was extremely lucky to get pregnant so quickly and I had a relatively easy pregnancy. And as I held our beautiful healthy daughter Ashley in my arms, I'd never been so thoroughly grateful to lose a game of Rock-Paper-Scissors.

But I'll tell you what I was pissed about losing ... SLEEP! Between Ashley being a difficult sleeper as an infant and then 6 months of the 'Terrible Twos,' I honestly wasn't sure I wanted to go through that whole thing again. I at least wanted to wait until we were in the clear from sleep deprivation and her toddler preposterousness until I considered another child.

And so, Erin was born when Ashley was four years old. We didn't find out if we were having a boy or girl for either pregnancy, so Ashley was thrilled to have a baby sister.

I'll never forget her smiling face as she jumped up and down in the hospital next to Erin's crib, looking at her little sister saying, "That's exactly what I wanted!"

And thankfully, Erin was a MUCH better sleeper.

RECOVERY & KIDS

I was sober for over 12 years before having children, and I can honestly say that parenting has taxed my sobriety like nothing before it. Yes, I do recognize how lucky I am – my kids are healthy and happy, I have a supportive partner, and on and on. But – FUCK – parenting is hard.

During the typical evening AA meeting times, I was busy digging baby shit out of my nails and attempting to get my kids to stay in bed. Luckily I was able to roll into motherhood with a strong foundation of recovery. I had a stockpile of AA meeting attendance, worked the steps, sorted out (most of) my demons, practiced good habits, and established solid friendships with supportive people both in and out of AA. After I had children, I found these opportunities became fewer and farther between – I simply had less time (and energy) to attend meetings and actively work on myself after having kids. Speaking of which...

Because I was not able to 'unwind with a glass of wine on the couch' at the end of the day, I had to figure out ways to take my parenting stress levels down a notch without chemicals. It was important for me to communicate my needs quickly and clearly when I felt overly tired, frustrated, and overwhelmed. Leaving things to fester would just lead to resentment and anger ... or using / self-medicating. I would know when I needed to lean on Mike, get out of the house and go for a walk, call a friend to talk, or – my personal favorite – get in a hot bath and read a trashy vampire novel. (Hey – don't judge! After fifteen years of parenting, this is still my preferred outlet.)

And while the sound of Ashley or Erin's laughter fills my soul, or hearing about something new they've learned brings me such pride, they are also a total time and energy suck! Yes, I said it. Therefore it was extremely important for Mike and I to make sure our partnership received the attention it deserved, even when the children were young ... maybe *especially* when the children were young. We made short vacations – just the two of us – a priority. Utah, Vegas, New York, and Florida to name some of our trips.

I remember one time in particular when Ashley was six and Erin was two, and we just had to get out of the damn house! Mike and I planned a last-minute trip to Miami, but the night before our early flight Ashley broke her wrist while scootering in the neighborhood. I had just gotten a spray tan, and if you're familiar with spray tans then you know you need to shower approximately 5 to 6 hours after getting one to stop the chemicals on your skin from continuing to darken. But there would be no shower for me because I was sitting in the emergency department at Children's Hospital of Philadelphia, slowly turning darker and darker before everyone's eyes while my daughter had a cast put on her arm.

With concern, we asked the doctors what to expect for her over the next couple of days. He said she might be a bit uncomfortable but nothing some Tylenol couldn't fix. Perfect. Around 1:00 a.m. on our way home, we stopped at a 24-hour CVS, got a bottle of children's Tylenol, and handed it to my mother-in-law who would be watching the girls while we were away. Then, a few short hours later, we boarded that glorious plane to Miami with no regrets (except for my painfully obvious fake tan).

Am I selfish? Are our 'adults only' trips together negatively impacting the growth, health, and needs of our children? Hell no. Since I never grew up seeing what a healthy adult relationship actually looked like, I believe one of the most important things I can do for my kids is SHOW them what a solid partnership looks like – and that includes my needs getting met. I want Ashley to know deep in her bones that her own feelings and desires still matter when she's 35 or 45 or 70. I want Erin to know – without hesitation or guilt – that she is allowed to enjoy a break, vacation, massage, or to be crazy and try something new at any age. And I am both fortunate and proud to serve as a solid example of a healthy person, partner, and parent for my kids.

Speaking of crazy... as the artist Seal said, *"We're never going to survive unless we get a little crazy."* If you were to meet me, you would quickly learn that in no way does being a parent or my lack of drinking / using drugs equate to me being boring – quite the opposite in fact.

For my 40th birthday, I had a raging 1980s themed party. (Yes, people with 20 years sober can rage). We had an amazing 1980s cover band from NYC, *Jessie's Girl*, entertain 120 of my closest friends, neighbors, and family. In preparation for this party, I decided to try something totally wild and new – I took months of drum lessons and surprised everybody at my party by drumming "Here I Go Again" by Whitesnake with Jessie's Girl on my 40th birthday night. Minds blown ... including my own.

After having so much fun together at the party, the band recommended we join them on a cruise they were booked on the following Spring – *The '80s Cruise.* Mike and I thought, "Why the hell not?!" and ten months later we boarded this magical ship. Non-stop live music, theme nights and costumes, hilarious people – an absolutely fantastic week (no drinking or drugs needed). Since 2017 *The '80s Cruise* has become an annual event for us, something we look forward to sharing with our marvelous and crazy '80s friends every March.

It's a miracle any of this happened. A fucking miracle. With support, I stayed (and stay) sober one day at a time, making all of this possible – not always easy, but possible. I have a life filled with deep relationships, kids, friendships, success and laughter. A life with serenity, joy, music, dancing, wild vacations, and memorable experiences.

And if you're lucky enough to be friends with me, you know you always have a designated driver ...

"Stay close to anything that makes you glad you are alive."
~ Hafiz

CHILL THE FUCK OUT

Mike and I are very fortunate to live in a wonderful school district which offers our family and kids excellent opportunities. I used to assume that feeling gratitude for our privileged place in the world was normal, an obvious reaction to such a blessed life. But I've come to realize over the years that many people are often looking towards the 'next thing,' having a 'grass is greener over there' perspective, not at all recognizing our privilege.

In 2018, Mike and I attended an end-of-the-school-year party with a group of parents and friends. Everyone was mingling and talking about the previous school year, summer plans and vacations, and upcoming fall sports for our kids – both at school and on travel teams.

"The earlier you get on the team the better," was the general assumption shared as parents talked about what sports they intended their children to play in the fall. I was listening to but not agreeing with the idea that every minute of kids' lives should be filled with activities. I believed that young kids should get to play freely versus starting competitive activities too soon.

The conversation then shifted to plans for high school and college – extracurriculars, sports, college applications. I was growing more aggravated – I mean, after all, our kids had just 'graduated' from fourth grade and these parents were stressing about college applications?

I entered the conversation with what I thought was the voice of reason: "I think maybe we can relax a little about all this future talk, yeah? I mean, they're still young and they should be playing around and having fun! I'm not really interested in stressing out my kid at ten years old. They have their entire adult life to be stressed out, right?" I kind of laughed and nodded, hoping somebody else would step in and back me up here.

I was met with silence and blank stares.

"Well, aren't you going to sign up Ashley for a travel team?" someone asked. "Didn't Mike play college lacrosse? Don't you want your girls to also play sports to get into college?" another followed. "You're not planning ahead now?"

And this was my brash response: "You all need to chill the fuck out. I don't think you understand how bad things in life can actually get. We live in a fairy tale land! Do you understand how hard it is for other people out there? We are all so fortunate and our kids are happy and healthy – let's just take that as a win, shall we?"

Again, silence and blank stares.

Looking back, I suppose I could have further – or perhaps more softly – explained myself and my unique perspective. I'd like to do that now...

I don't know what will happen for my kids in sports, high school, college or later, but I do know that I don't want them to experience any of the bad things that happened to me. So maybe I should have asked these parents:

- Have you ever been to rehab? Have you ever been to two?!

- Have you ever gotten into a fist fight over the last rock of crack?

- Have you ever been sexually assaulted?

- Have you ever taken your clothes out of your suitcase to cover yourself while sleeping in the back of a random car because you're homeless?

- Have you ever arrived to class in your stinky greasy uniform with your stinky greasy hair because you didn't have time to change between your restaurant shift and microbiology lab?

Again, things could be so much worse. I will choose my kids' safety and joy over societal expectations ... every single time.

Because of my experiences, I find I see things differently – maybe with a different scope or awareness. And I understand that a healthy life is a gift, a blessing – something I may have earned but no one is given. Life can change in an instant, and I'm grateful that I have been trained to make the next right decision, one step at a time, to (hopefully) pick up the pieces.

I'm grateful for discomfort – because I know I can choose for it to lead to growth.

I'm hopeful I can teach these things to my girls so they can see how green the grass already is right below their feet.

So please – ground yourself, look around, find something beautiful, hug the people you love, and remember to please chill the fuck out.

"Don't sweat the small stuff... and it's all small stuff."

~ Richard Carlson

HITTING A WALL

Something happened in March of 2020 – the Coronavirus Pandemic. Ring a bell? Mike and I had literally just stepped off our 4th *'80s Cruise* when the world shut down. For us, like everybody, there was no escape. The kids were in the house – all the time. There was no going out, no socializing, no date nights, no massages, no fucking anything! There was no relief. Certainly not for me.

Many of you had *some* relief – I watched you pour the relief down your throats every afternoon. It was probably the first time in over 20 years that I felt jealous knowing you could drink and I could not. I had no option for escape as I lived in this scary new reality. So ... I started crunching.

While you had wine, I found relief in loud, endless crunching of potato chips – bags and bags of potato chips. It was as if I had hooked a potato chip bag to my face using a bungee cord behind my neck. At any point during the day, you could lick my fingers and they would taste salty.

I knew it was time to stop when I could no longer fit into my most stretchy leggings. Like many of you, I gained weight during the pandemic, and I would have to work my ass off to lose it – especially considering that I was now in the throes of perimenopause. Jesus, that could be a whole other book – marriage, parenting, working ... all while experiencing the symptoms of perimenopause right in the middle of Covid? Women are superheroes.

When COVID started in 2020 I had been sober for 24 years. Twenty-Four Years! And hands down, those first six months of the pandemic were the hardest months of sobriety for me since my first six months sober in 1996. I found myself restless, distracted, uncomfortable being in the 'now.' Mind you, the 'now' really sucked for everyone, but – was something more going on for me?

COVID was an excellent reminder that this disease of addiction was still alive inside me, whispering to me, offering the readily-attainable option to escape reality. It was always patiently waiting for me to give up the sobriety struggle and return to the seductive blur zone. And there were definitely days and moments over those 24 years where I craved the beautiful fuzzy feeling drugs or alcohol provided me. I can almost feel my throat burning, eyes watering, and shoulders relaxing now. But thankfully I'd been well trained, and my integrity had become stronger than the pull for substances. So, to my ever-lurking disease I say, *"Fuck you. Pass the potato chips."*

In February of 2021, I celebrated my 25th sobriety anniversary on an online AA meeting, followed by an ice cream cake my husband and girls bought for me with a big, gold "25" stuck in the top.

Recognizing 25 years sober was a surreal milestone for me – highly emotional, almost unbelievable.

How the hell did I get here?

I hope by now you know the answer ...

|| PROGRESS, NOT PERFECTION ||

"Wherever you go, there you are."

~ Thomas à Kempis

I've spent almost three decades digging through that trash can in my soul. I've dealt with a lot of smelly stuff, pulled it out, looked closely at it, and then gotten rid of it. Let me be clear, just because I was sober didn't mean I was perfect in my 20s and 30s. Even in sobriety I made mistakes – adding trash to the trash can – which I would later have to pull out and deal with. But that's all part of this crazy trip, right? As I learned in AA, it's about progress, not perfection.

So, what am I digging into today?

THE FIGHTER

A favorite quote of mine that I first heard in early recovery was *"If it's not moving, it's probably dead."* I think it was the pandemic which allowed me to notice that in some ways, my life – my recovery – had perhaps ... stagnated.

I started to wonder what character defects I still carried in my trash can – or what new ones might have developed over the years that I was currently blind to see. I mean, do we at some point just look and find our trash can empty – no more growth or realization or healing required? Doubtful. Highly doubtful! And for some reason I actually valued (maybe even welcomed) digging in and dealing with parts of me that weren't feeling whole.

Because I've always been better at active 'doing' over passive 'feeling,' I looked for guidance and support as I opened the lid. I got involved with a life coach who happened to specialize in a specific therapy tool called Integrated Family Systems (IFS). I had no idea what I was in for with this woman, but I loved that she regularly had me doing active work – self-inquiry, meditation, writing – exploring my inner self and my reactions to people in my life.

My coach helped me to identify particular 'hamster wheels' that I couldn't seem to step off – certain cycles and patterns I had which were not helpful or healthy. And the main pattern was my identification with the Fighter – remember her? She was still looking for and fighting battles every day. I've since learned that the Fighter is often dominant in so many of us – she wants to defeat something and feel victorious, she wants to be a leader and hungers to be successful. But the Fighter lacks softness. (Ouch, yeah, sounds like me...)

Now that I see this aspect of myself, I'm learning how to sometimes give the Fighter in me time off. That way, maybe childhood Tracy can pop up – the softer Tracy who would happily run around my dad's farm, enthusiastically play with my friends, or snuggle with Ruffles.

I'm working on the idea that sometimes 'making the next right decision' can actually mean doing nothing at all – dare I say, even kicking back and resting? Along with teaching my beautiful daughters the value of grit and working towards success, I also want to model elements of softness and resting and peace. Something that, up to this point, I fear I have failed at.

My husband loves this quote by Matthew Kelly: *"Most people overestimate what they can do in a day, and underestimate what they can accomplish in a year."* And as Mike and I were discussing what I was working on in my book the other day he said something to me I had never thought of before. With pride in his eyes, he looked at me and said: "Tracy ... it took you only six years from the time you were homeless to attending an Ivy League University. You are proof that miracles can be accomplished."

Little by little, I am hoping I can learn to give the Fighter a moment off here and there. She deserves it, she has worked miracles. And I am excited to get to know this softer Tracy. I am excited to see what new miracles she will produce.

BODY IMAGE

I still struggle with the occasional whisper in my head telling me I look fat or my thighs are too big. I definitely struggle with some element of what's clinically called *body dysmorphic disorder*, where I don't see myself or my shape the way other people see me. Like, literally – my eyeballs and my visual cortex play tricks on me. And now it feels like an uphill battle since I'm going through some hormonal changes – a battle I will lose to gravity, chemistry, loss of collagen, and muscle mass. (Well, that's fucking depressing.)

This negative body self-talk is definitely something I would like to work on ... because it sucks. I would never talk to a friend the way I talk about myself in my head. I would never even say these words out loud for someone to hear! So why, if I truly do love and respect myself, why can I be such an asshole when it specifically comes to my size?

More trash to sort ... but I'm up for it. Progress, not perfection.

BEING 15 AGAIN

My oldest daughter is 15 years old – she is at the age where I started to break. She is the warmest, funniest, most empathic person in the room. I wonder if I was like her before I fell... though her situation is entirely different than my life was at fifteen – or for any of the years before then as well.

But there is still a part of me that braces myself, wondering if (or when) my kids may make adverse life-altering choices, wondering if I've passed on my addiction gene at some level. I suppose all I can do is set an example for my daughters, be forthcoming regarding my experiences, and guide them as best I can while constantly, consciously losing this game of tug-of-war with them as they beautifully grow up.

But honestly, this parenting thing is scary as shit! I don't really know what I'm doing. Just doing the best I can with the information I have ... and hoping for the best.

ACME

After 27 years, I can still see it. I can still see that beat-up Toyota sedan behind the ACME grocery store. I can still remember crawling into that back seat feeling angry, terrified, lost ... and incredibly cold. Though the landscape has changed in the past quarter century, now flanked by other stores and restaurants, the ACME remains. It sits not five minutes from where my family and I live today. And with it, so does my memory of that fitful night's sleep in January of 1996.

But this ACME, this location, this memory, does not hold pain for me anymore. It holds promise. I see that girl in the back of the Toyota and my heart breaks for all that she had been through. She made bad decisions in response to bad circumstances. I want to hug that addict/alcoholic and let her know there's something bigger and better inside of her. It's going to hurt. It's going to take time. But little by little you - sweet innocent girl - you will become a lot.

DEATH ... OR LIFE

According to Oliver Burkeman, *"The average human life span is absurdly, terrifyingly, insultingly short [about 4,000 weeks on average]."* If this is true, at 47 years old I've now made the turnaround and I'm headed home – I've got less time ahead of me than I've already lived behind me. I suppose this fact can either be terrifying or encouraging. Luckily, I have a choice. So with this in mind, what do I want to do with the time remaining?

In a 2013 article by Tim Urban, he explains how our lives might be a full picture, but we are living our 'everyday' in the pixels of that larger picture. That really hit me ...

I feel like I often get wrapped up in the stupid, everyday shit. I know these are things that must get done – dinner, carpooling, laundry, etc. – but I want to make sure my checking off the endless 'to-do' list doesn't rule me. If that's the case, I'm going to need to continue healing the intense action and results-driven Fighter and work towards not being so hard on myself. I want the pixels of my life to be mindful and contented. I want the pixels to be colorful as I love the shit out of my husband and kids and friends.

I know that I will keep moving forward, baby-stepping, working to leave the world a little better. I know that some days will be better than others and life is going to continue to unfold – hopefully good, sometimes bad. But I've learned through recovery to embrace life on life's terms.

For me that means no drinky-poo and no tokey-poo. I don't get to numb out the edges – and that's okay. The view from here is pretty damn good.

"It's not about how hard you hit. It's about how hard you can get hit and keep moving forward – how much you can take and keep moving forward.

That's how winning is done!"

~ Rocky Balboa (Sylvester Stallone)

Acknowledgements

Acknowledgment

|| ACKNOWLEDGEMENTS ||

"A diamond is proof that you sometimes have to go through a great deal of pressure before you can shine."

~ Matshona Dhliwayo

To Mike. You helped me with every word of this book, and we both know you are now addicted to the 'thesaurus' feature on my laptop. This process was certainly an adventure, and I apologize for how moody I was at home as I wrote the chapters that brought back a lot of pain. Thank you for putting up with me and not judging me when I came downstairs to get my third bowl of potato chips. I truly adore the shit out of you. (P.S. 12 to 18 months...)

To Ashley and Erin, my girls. I cannot express how fantastic you both are and how proud of you I am. Yes, I'm your biased mom, but for realz, no cap, you both slay. You are both growing up so fast and I am lowkey freaking out a little bit. Please don't ghost me as you get older. I'm not your opp and I'm also not mid. I know you are fire and you got rizz, but let me do a vibe check here and there, and we can spill the tea. kk? I mean, IYKYK.

To my mom. I want to thank you for your enduring love for me, your belief that I could / would change, and all of your efforts – physical, financial, emotional – to get me sober. As a mom myself now, I cannot imagine the pain you went through and the strength it took to not let me come home after Minnesota. I don't know how you possibly carried the death of your father, the death of our dog, AND my addiction during that terrible time. Mom - I would not be here without you and the efforts you made to help me.

To my dad. I'll never forget watching Tommy Boy while eating hoagies with you in your den. We were doing nothing at all, and yet I knew something was changing. I vividly remember sitting with you on your boat dock when I was grown, watching you hold Erin in your lap and lovingly playing with her little toes. I'll never forget the day you received your terminal brain cancer diagnosis, or sitting by your bed saying all those powerful words we never seem to say until the end. I had the honor of watching you, with such calm bravery, ask to please leave the hospital and go home for your final days. How I miss sitting with you on your front porch enjoying that beautiful view... saying nothing at all.

To Pop-Pop. I was the worst and you deserved so much better. I'm so sorry for being such a horrible teenager to you, Mum-Mum, and mom when all you wanted to do was help. I still have your sweater – the one you wore the last time I saw you. Every so often when I see it in my 'memories' box, I smell it and hug it and cry. I hope, wherever you are, that you know I'm ok now – better than ok! I'm safe, happy, successful. I have a wonderful life and family. And maybe when I see you again, we could just sit there for a little bit and watch Lawrence Welk together... Oh, and I'm sorry for making your car smell like vomit.

To Mum-Mum, you deserve a big shoutout. For several agonizing years you watched your daughter go through a long, difficult divorce while sharing your home with mom and me (and Ruffles). And then you had to helplessly watch me as I dropped out of college and became a homeless drug addict. All this followed by the sudden loss of your husband – and through all of that you never once complained. Never once. You put on that Fire & Ice lipstick and those black pumps and showed up for us every day. I am so grateful you got to see me get sober and graduate from college, get my Master's degree, get a good job, and get married. I was honored to sit on the side of your bed and hold your hand as you passed on. I hope you told Pop-Pop all these things when you re-connected with him. I love you both.

To Dave. I could not have done these past 27+ years without you as part of this process. You are my no-questions-asked, where/when-do-you-need-me, bury-a-body friend. I love you.

To E. You were the first I told about the idea of doing this book, and you have supported me throughout. Encouraging me, giving feedback, there for me when I dug into the hardest parts of my memories. Thank you for your friendship. (And, no, Isis is not the name of a hurricane...)

To my high school girlfriends, my college friends, my neighborhood 'moms,' my 'green' friends and my fantastic 80s crew. You rock!!! I'm so lucky to have you all in my life.

To Maggie Poulos of Mix-Tape Media. Thank you for your friendship since 8th grade, and thank you for your professional PR help and guidance to make this book a reality. http://www.mixtape-media.com/

To Scott Reynolds, our friend and amazing photographer. I love my author photo – you captured me perfectly. Thank you! (Instagram: @scotttslens)

To Natalie, DeeDee and The Moxi Group for all of my social media, well, everything! I am the worst at this, and thankfully you are the freaking best. https://www.themoxigroup.com/

To John Selby. I learned so much about writing, dialogue, emotional depth, and commas. I could not have brought this book to life without your direction. https://www.johnselby.com/

To my copy editor (J. Flowers), cover designer (H-Izz Design), publisher, distributor, and on and on. Damn – writing and publishing a book isn't easy! I am grateful to have worked with people who not only know what the hell they are doing, but are also outstanding.

To Richard ... I win.

"The rain is nothing to fear when you become the storm."
~ Dee Snyder

|| ABOUT THE AUTHOR ||

Tracy Viola was born on Philadelphia's Main Line where she still resides with her husband, two daughters and her calico cat, Olivia. She holds a BA from Villanova University and a Master's degree in Counseling Psychology from Temple University. Tracy has been continuously sober since February of 1996, and has been a sought-after speaker by schools and recovery centers.

Pretty Wrecked is her first book.

www.tracyviolaauthor.com

Printed in the USA
CPSIA information can be obtained
at www.ICGtesting.com
JSHW010940060124
54831JS00009B/103